T0114446

THE PSYCHOLOGY OF WORKING LIFE

What motivates us to do a good job? When does the pressure of work impact upon our health and well-being? How can employers choose the right candidates?

The Psychology of Working Life shows how, whether we like it or not, the way we work, and our feelings about it, play a fundamental role in overall well-being. From the use of psychometrics in recruiting the right candidate, to making working life more efficient, the book illustrates how work in industrialized societies continues to be founded upon core psychological ideas.

Motivation and job satisfaction have become recognized as key to job design and *The Psychology of Working Life* suggests that changing the way we work can impact on our stress levels, overall health, and productivity.

Toon Taris is Professor of Work and Organisational Psychology at Utrecht University in the Netherlands. He has a particular interest in worker stress and health.

THE PSYCHOLOGY OF EVERYTHING

The Psychology of Everything is a series of books which debunk the myths and pseudo-science surrounding some of life's biggest questions.

The series explores the hidden psychological factors that drive us, from our sub-conscious desires and aversions, to the innate social instincts handed to us across the generations. Accessible, informative, and always intriguing, each book is written by an expert in the field, examining how research-based knowledge compares with popular wisdom, and illustrating the potential of psychology to enrich our understanding of humanity and modern life.

Applying a psychological lens to an array of topics and contemporary concerns – from sex to addiction to conspiracy theories – The Psychology of Everything will make you look at everything in a new way.

Titles in the series:

The Psychology of Grief
Richard Gross

The Psychology of Sex
Meg-John Barker

The Psychology of Dieting
Jane Ogden

The Psychology of Performance
Stewart T. Cotterill

The Psychology of Trust
Ken J. Rotenberg

The Psychology of Working Life
Toon Taris

The Psychology of Conspiracy Theories
Jan-Willem van Prooijen

The Psychology of Addiction
Jenny Svanberg

The Psychology of Fashion
Carolyn Mair

The Psychology of Gardening
Harriet Gross

The Psychology of Gender
Gary W. Wood

For further information about this series please visit www.thepsychologyofeverything.co.uk

THE PSYCHOLOGY OF WORKING LIFE

TOON TARIS

Routledge
Taylor & Francis Group

LONDON AND NEW YORK

First published 2018
by Routledge
2 Park Square, Milton Park, Abingdon, Oxon OX14 4RN

and by Routledge
711 Third Avenue, New York, NY 10017

Routledge is an imprint of the Taylor & Francis Group, an informa business

© 2018 Toon Taris

The right of Toon Taris to be identified as author of this work has
been asserted by him in accordance with sections 77 and 78 of the
Copyright, Designs and Patents Act 1988.

All rights reserved. No part of this book may be reprinted or
reproduced or utilised in any form or by any electronic, mechanical,
or other means, now known or hereafter invented, including
photocopying and recording, or in any information storage or
retrieval system, without permission in writing from the publishers.

Trademark notice: Product or corporate names may be trademarks or
registered trademarks, and are used only for identification and
explanation without intent to infringe.

British Library Cataloguing-in-Publication Data
A catalogue record for this book is available from the British Library

Library of Congress Cataloging-in-Publication Data
A catalog record for this book has been requested

ISBN: 978-1-138-20724-0 (hbk)
ISBN: 978-1-138-20725-7 (pbk)
ISBN: 978-1-315-46273-8 (ebk)

Typeset in Joanna
by Apex CoVantage, LLC

CONTENTS

ACKNOWLEDGEMENTS

Many people contributed in some form to this book – too many to thank them all. I am especially grateful to the management of Utrecht University's strategic theme Institutions for a Top Researcher grant that allowed me to write part of this text. Obviously, this book could not have been written without the findings and ideas of many researchers in psychology, economics, sociology and medicine. Two of them – Michiel Kompier and Wilmar Schaufeli – deserve a special mention: over the years, both of you have been a source of inspiration to me. A big thank you to Paul, Yvonne, Ton, Jasper, Marit, Jos and Pieter (both of them) for providing material used in Chapter 7. My wife, Inge, came up with the example given in the last section of Chapter 4 and lovingly supported me while I was writing this text. Finally, I dedicate this book to Marit, Kiki and Crispijn, without whom this book would not have been written. This book is my answer to their nagging question, *Dad, now what do you actually do when you are at work?*

1

WHAT WE TALK ABOUT WHEN WE TALK ABOUT WORK

In 1848, Karl Marx and Friedrich Engels published their *Communist Manifesto*. Reacting to the social and working circumstances of the working class, they stated that

> Owing to the extensive use of machinery, and to the division of labour, the work of the proletarians [workers] has lost all individual character, and, consequently, all charm for the workman . . . it is only the most simple, most monotonous, and most easily acquired knack, that is required of him.[1]

This quote may suggest otherwise, but working is not necessarily one of the rotten facts of life. For example, in the classic Donald Duck story *Monsterville* by cartoonist Carl Barks, the brilliant inventor Gyro Gearloose persuades the city council to turn Duckburg into an automated city in which no human effort is needed to make it run. However, the citizens quickly discover that doing nothing all day makes their lives empty, boring and unhappy: even the toys play by themselves.[2] Granted, work can be exhausting, frustrating and deadening, and it does take away time that could otherwise be spent on all sorts of fun activities. However, it is hard to imagine us leading a satisfying life without work, not only because work provides us with an income but also because it can be a source of joy, structure, status, challenge, social contact, meaning and purpose, as well a means to impact the lives of others positively. As US President Theodore Roosevelt put it, "A mere life of ease is not in the end a very satisfactory life".[3]

This book is about work, working and the role of psychology therein. Its first main thesis is that the way we work today is not only due to technological advances and economic considerations regarding the most efficient and profitable way to employ the three major factors of production (capital, natural resources and labour) for producing goods or services. Rather, *the way we work is also to a large degree due to our views on the best way to put these factors — especially* labour *— to good use*. Man has certainly not always worked in factories and offices or at home, performing well-defined tasks following strict rules and procedures and using tools and machinery tailored to these tasks, taking away "all charm for the workman", as Marx and Engels maintained. Although there is no point in denying that economic and technological considerations have been (and still are) major drivers of change in the way we deal with labour (i.e. the way we work), they alone are insufficient to understand how people perform best at work, why some people perform better than others while holding the same job, why they are happy or unhappy with their jobs, et cetera.

At this point, it is useful to note that it would be wrong to assume that technological innovations unavoidably and irreversibly lead to corresponding changes in the way we work. History has shown that innovations are sometimes rejected in spite of having clear advantages as compared with older technologies, or that older technologies persist in the presence of more promising alternatives. Examples of the first include the disappearance of wheeled vehicular transportation in Northern Africa between 300 and 700 AD, replacing wagon and cart with the camel and, more recently, the termination of Boeing's supersonic passenger jet development programme in 1971 by the US Senate (which was intended as a competitor of the British-French Concorde and the Soviet Tupolev TU-144 supersonic airliners). Examples of the latter include the re-introduction of wood stoves as a form of "green energy" and the continuing use of the QWERTY keyboard layout (which was allegedly devised to make fast typing difficult as mechanical typewriters would easily jam) rather than the more ergonomic DVORAK layout. Indeed, positive developments are sometimes *reversed* in favour of functionally awkward and inefficient technologies, for example consider the use of laptop computers, tablets and even mobile phones instead of devices with full-size keyboards and screens. Clearly, in the face of the availability of new technology, we have a choice whether and how we will let new technological features impact our lives and the way we work.[4]

Building on the assumption that the way we work is to a large degree due to our views on the best way to put labour to good use, the second main thesis of this book is that *the way we work is an important factor in determining the "outcomes" of a job*, for the worker (e.g. in terms of motivation, health, well-being and performance), his or her environment (e.g. their work team) as well as the organization he or she works for (including its efficiency, profitability and overall performance). This implies that the choices we make regarding the organization of work have real and important consequences for both individual workers and for society as a whole, in tangible financial terms as well as in terms of human well-being and happiness. Therefore, it is important for all of us – whether we are workers who are subjected to the choices of others as to how we must work, professionals who affect the way others must work (e.g. as human resource professionals, supervisors or employers) or students aspiring to become such professionals – to understand how these choices regarding the organization of work affect workers, their well-being and behaviour.

Its third main thesis is that *there is nothing intrinsically bad about working hard*, provided that the job does not have lasting adverse effects on the worker. For instance, while working with carcinogenic or poisonous substances may sometimes be unavoidable, utmost care should be taken in preventing that doing so affects worker health negatively. Similarly, working excessively hard (all work, no play) will make Jack (or Jill, for that matter) not only a dull but also a stressed and burned-out boy (or girl). Thus, there should be a balance between work and high performance on the one hand and health and recovery from work on the other, to maintain what may be called *sustainable* performance.[5]

The final thesis of this book is that *taking a psychological view on working life* – which we construe as the choices made regarding the organization of work and their consequences for the health, well-being and behaviour of the workers involved, and the performance of workers and organizations – *is essential in understanding how the balance between being highly productive and remaining healthy and happy can be optimized*. Specifically, psychologists and psychologically-inspired management researchers (and I am talking about the academics here, not the gurus) have generated a wealth of research in these years, containing many useful insights in the areas of work organization, work motivation, occupational health and work performance. I am convinced that work design is (and should be!) as much a matter of psychology as it is of technology and economics, which is the main impetus for this book in the first place.

Against this background, this book is built around two broad questions. The first is "why do we work the way we work?", focusing on the insights, theories and findings that have guided the design of the workplace. To some degree, the answer to this question requires taking a historical perspective, as yesteryear's undisputed truths have sometimes been superseded by more recent and conflicting insights – yet continue to affect the way jobs are designed. The second question is "how can work performance and worker well-being be optimized – and at what costs?", referring to the applied potential of this subject as well as to the need to maintain a healthy balance between high performance and worker health on the longer term. Although in the subsequent chapters of this book, I refer to these questions only in passing, in its concluding Chapter 7, I return to these issues and discuss how the insights presented in this book are relevant to these questions.

TALKING ABOUT WORK . . .

In everyday life, the noun "work" refers to "activity involving mental or physical effort done in order to achieve a result . . . a means of earning income".[6] This definition highlights two important facets of the term. First, work consists of *goal-directed* activity, rather than of a set of more or less random actions that may, perhaps, at some time in the future, bring about a desired outcome. Specifically, actions at work are intended to bring about a particular intended result, usually the production of goods or services. Consequently, actions at work are usually *planned and coordinated* to fit well with other workers' actions and the aims of the company. To this aim, the tasks to be conducted at work often follow particular routines, guidelines and procedures and are frequently conducted with the help of computer programmes, tools and machinery that are especially developed to allow the worker to achieve the intended goal. To maximize the ease at which the worker is able to achieve the goals of the job, a particular type and level of education and training is often required.

Second, the activities conducted at work *require mental and/or physical effort and this effort is compensated in some way*, usually in the form of a monetary reward. It is conceivable that this reward is not received immediately or takes a non-monetary form. For example, students may take an unpaid internship as part of their college duties in exchange for study credits or to gain valuable skills and experience that will help them find a paid job after graduation. Such internships may be considered as an investment that will hopefully reap its returns in the future.

Note that the requirement that work involves a compensation of one's effort means that unpaid work (such as household activities) is not classified as "work", although these activities may be very similar to those conducted by others as part of their paid jobs. Taking care of your own young children is not classified as work. However, if you frequently take care of *other* parents' offspring, it is likely that you are either a babysitter or an employee of a day-care centre and that you receive some sort of pay in return: that is, you are *working*. Thus, the difference between work and other activities is whether the person conducting the tasks receives some sort of monetary reward; it does not reside in the type of tasks that are conducted. The principles discussed in Chapter 2 concerning the optimal design of tasks can therefore often be applied to both work and household activities.

IN THE BEGINNING . . .

Although since the 1950s many scholars have studied working life from a psychological perspective, systematic thinking about the way work tasks can be conducted best started much earlier. An early example is what has come to be known as the *Hippocratic corpus*, consisting of a collection of about 60 books written by various Greek authors from the 5th to the 3rd century BC. These books document ancient Greek medical knowledge, providing doctors with detailed procedures and guidelines as to how specific complaints (such as haemorrhoids, ulcers or fractures) should be treated. Here is how physicians should behave while treating a patient:

> Do everything in a calm and orderly manner, concealing most things from the patient while treating him. Give what encouragement is required cheerfully and calmly, diverting his attention from his own circumstances; on one occasion rebuke him harshly and strictly, on another console him with solicitude and attention, revealing nothing of his future or present condition.[7]

Similarly, the Roman legion was organized according to clear and simple principles. Positions in this organization were well-defined in terms of the tasks to be conducted and how these tasks should be executed. Several manuals described how various parts of this army should operate in specific situations. Based on older texts, the Roman writer Vegetius published *De Re Militari* ("On military matters") around 390 BC. In this short treatise, he discussed the organization, equipment and drill of the Roman legions, including topics such as the selection and training of recruits, the organization of the legion and how to stab the enemy. For example, Roman officers were advised to prevent mutiny among the troops by making

> it their business to keep up so strict a discipline as to leave [the troops] no room to harbour any thoughts but of submission and obedience. Let them be constantly employed either in field days

or in the inspection of their arms. . . . They should be frequently called by roll and trained to be exact in the observance of every signal . . . let all this be continually repeated and let them be often kept under arms till they are tired. . . . All the different kinds of troops thus trained and exercised in their quarters will find themselves inspired with emulation for glory and eagerness for action when they come to take the field . . . a soldier who has proper confidence in his own skill and strength, entertains no thought of mutiny.[8]

Interestingly, this quote not only shows how Roman officers were advised to behave while on duty, but also demonstrates that Vegetius had a keen eye for the psychological consequences of training and exercise. Keeping the troops busy with all sorts of drills and training activities would not only rob them of the energy and initiative needed to start a rebellion, but it would also increase their skills, strength, self-confidence and eagerness for action. Thus, by keeping their troops engaged, Roman officers were assumed to be able to turn them into compliant yet skilled and motivated fighting machines.

As these examples show, early thinking on how particular tasks should be conducted relied on common sense, tradition, moral axioms, long-standing historical practices and laymen's psychological insights. A more scientific (i.e. more rigorous, systematic and empirical) approach to examining work and its effects on worker performance and well-being emerged much later. The 1500s saw the publication of Georgius Agricola's De Re Metallica (On the nature of metals), an influential book on the art and science of mining. Agricola discussed the technical details of mining, but – being the town physician of Chemnitz in Saxony, then an important mining area – he was also interested in the occupational diseases typical of miners. Not only did his book cover "the ailments and accidents of miners", but Agricola also discussed methods to prevent these, such as wearing face veils to guard miners from inhaling mining dust. Moreover, he recommended that mines should be operated in a 5-day work week with three 8-hour shifts per day; no miner should work two or more shifts per day because of the increasing risk of occupational injury. Moreover, in line with the third main thesis of this book that performance should be sustainable, Agricola states that "we should always devote more care to maintaining our health . . . than to making profits" – ideas that sound surprisingly modern.[9] Similarly, first published in 1700 in Modena, Italy, Bernardino Ramazzini's seminal book titled *De Morbis Artificum Diatriba* ("On the diseases of workers") documented the typical illnesses occurring among workers in 52 occupations. Ramazzini argued that occupational diseases could result from four sources: handling minerals and metals; inhaling toxins; being exposed to fluids such as water, milk and alcoholic beverages; and taking unnatural positions or holding positions for long periods.[10] The works of Ramazzini and Agricola constituted the beginning of the discipline now known as occupational medicine.

The industrial revolution of the late 18th and early 19th century marked an unprecedented transition towards new manufacturing processes that drew heavily on the use of water power and steam power. These manufacturing processes changed from artisanal piece-by-piece production to mass production. The economic system itself was transformed into that of industrial capitalism. Large mills and factories were erected that often employed hundreds or even thousands of workers: men, women and children. Thousands of miles of canals, roads and railways were built to transport raw materials to these factories and mills and the goods they produced to the stores where they were sold. Workers found new employment into these mills and factories, causing cities to burgeon. This fierce industrialization process was not without success: according to one author, in Britain the income per person (an indicator of the standard of living) roughly doubled during the period 1760–1860. Expressed in 1970 US dollars, this income increased from about $400 in 1760 to $430 in 1800, to $500 in 1830, to $800 in 1860.[11]

Yet, in spite of this doubling of the per-person income, working and living conditions in these times remained harsh, at least to modern eyes.[12] Factory and mine owners sought for ways to discipline and control their workforce through a system of long working hours (working 12 to 14 hours a day was common), cruel discipline (adult workers were frequently hit with leather straps; children were sometimes punished by nailing their ears to a table) and fines for talking or whistling during work times, leaving the room without permission or for producing less than was agreed upon. Indeed, miners could end a week's work owing money to the mine owner if their ore tubs were underweight.[13,14] Overall, the circumstances at work did little to motivate workers to exhaust themselves for their employers, and it is hardly surprising that in the middle of the 19th century workers became more and more susceptible to the rhetoric of revolutionaries such as Marx and Engels. Therefore, it became increasingly important to the owners of mills and factories to reflect on how they could keep their workers from revolting and motivate them to work hard instead. If not discipline, low wages, fines and excessively long working hours, then what would work? This is the point in time where the art and science of designing workplaces and jobs — that is the conscious shaping of people's experiences at work, or their working life — started off. Traditionally, the way people worked had mainly if not exclusively been the result of technological and economic developments, but by the end of the 19th century, what we would now call psychological considerations became increasingly important.

2

HARDER, BETTER, FASTER, STRONGER
The rationalization of working life

Surrounded by a spacious garden and hidden from the public by lus-
cious green walls of shrubs and trees, 8410 St. Martins Lane is a large
Georgian mansion in the wealthy part of Philadelphia, Pennsylvania.
Built in 1903 and aptly named after the immense 100-year old box
hedges planted by its first owner, Boxley initially gained fame for its
gardens. Sadly, the box did not strike root well and have long disappeared. Today, Boxley is better known as the house that Frederick
Winslow Taylor built for himself and his family. At the time, Taylor had
acquired a solid reputation as an engineer, an inventor and a management consultant *avant-la-lettre* who was the intellectual father of the
scientific management method, an approach that intended to address
the pressing issue of worker productivity using scientific insights.

A MAN, A MISSION

Born in 1856 into a well-to-do Philadelphia Quaker family, Taylor's
parents enrolled him in the prestigious Phillips Exeter Academy as
a preparation for Harvard Law School. Unfortunately, due to either
undetected astigmatism or (in his own words) "studying too hard",
while at Exeter he experienced serious headache problems forcing
him to drop out, abandoning the legal career his parents had in mind

for him. Instead, he took on an apprenticeship as a machinist and a pattern maker in a local pump factory owned by friends of the family. After three years, he moved on to a job as a lathe operator at Midvale Steel (merged in 1956 with Heppenstall Steel Company of Pittsburgh) elsewhere in Philadelphia. After having been on the job for only two months and perhaps due to his connections with Midvale Steel's management, he was promoted to gang-boss (foreman) over the lathe operators at the age of 23.

At the time, workers were less subject to the power of management than to the power wielded by foremen, who operated largely independently from their superiors. Managers were glad to leave matters in the hands of their foremen, who hired, fired and disciplined the rough, tough and uncivilized workers at their own discretion. Corruption was not uncommon: foremen routinely sold jobs to workers for $5 (a week's worth of working) to as much as $25, bosses were "treated" on pay day and cases of beer and boxes of cigars were mysteriously sent to their homes, bills paid.[1] In return for bribing their foremen, workers obtained a certain degree of control over their working conditions as well as some protection against managers' and owners' interests in having the most output for the least pay. In this system, foremen were obviously not particularly concerned with the management's objective of achieving maximum profit and efficiency, and they tended to form alliances with workers against management. For example, as elsewhere at the time, at Midvale most workers were paid on piece rate – the harder they worked, the more they earned. But only up to a point where the boss decided that a worker was making too much money, where he would promptly cut the rate. If all workers would be earning $2 and one worker would work hard enough to earn $3, it would become evident that the other workers were slacking and that the rate was set too high, lowering the motivation to work hard. Thus, in this system efficiency was achieved by setting the piece rate as low as possible. This implied that for workers it was important to limit output. Everyone knew that if the output would be too high, pay rates would be cut and all would suffer. So every form of pressure and persuasion went towards ensuring that no worker worked much faster than the other workers: foremen, as overseers, were instrumental in this practice.[2]

Frederick Taylor's personal aim as a gang-boss was to change these practices. As a former apprentice and lathe operator, he knew that as a rule, workers restricted their output by not working as hard as would be possible. Having been promoted to foreman, his intention was to get more work out of his former co-workers. It is not entirely clear why he decided to do so. On one account, the fact that his family was friends with Midvale's management may have been an important factor: in terms of his ancestry and social status, Taylor was more of a manager than of a worker, causing him to side with the company's management. On another account, his fast promotion to gang-boss may have made him determined to prove that he was worth his mettle by getting out more work from his men. Finally, Taylor may honestly have believed that by making his men work harder, he was doing everyone a favour. The men would earn more, the management would make a better profit, output would increase, the standards of living would improve, indeed, society as a whole would benefit: who could be against that?

Initially, Taylor attempted to persuade his former colleagues (or "friends", as he called them) to work harder – to no avail. Could the lack of productivity increases perhaps be due to a lack of skills of the workers? Being a machinist and a lathe operator himself, he showed them how to do their jobs properly – to no avail. He fired unproductive workers and hired others – to no avail. Finally, Taylor cut rates in half. That worked: productivity rose. However, so did the number of accidents at work. Almost every day accidents afflicted machines around the shop, forcing workers to remain idle. The men said that this was because their "fool foreman . . . was driving the men and the machines beyond their proper limit". However, Taylor suspected that these accidents were planned by the workers. He instigated a system of fines where the person in charge of the machine would either pay for its repair if an accident occurred, or be sent away.[3] After three years of this, Taylor succeeded in getting his men to do a "fair's day work" – but, quite understandably, at the sacrifice of the relationships with his former "friends". As Taylor noted when looking back at his time at Midvale,

> It is a horrid life for any man to live, not to be able to look any workman in the face all day long without seeing hostility there and feeling that every man around is his virtual enemy. . . . I made up my mind either to get out of the business entirely and go in some other line of work or to find some remedy for this unbearable condition.[4]

THE PRINCIPLES OF SCIENTIFIC MANAGEMENT

The remedy that Taylor ultimately developed during his 30-year period of working for and with various companies was *scientific management*. Not inclined to being overly respectful to others, Taylor did not make it a secret that his approach rested on two assumptions. The first was that workers were lazy:

> Instead of using every effort to turn out the largest possible amount of work, in a majority of cases [a worker] deliberately plans to do as little as he safely can . . . deliberately working slowly so as to avoid doing a full day's work . . . is almost universal.[5]

Taylor's second assumption was that workers were stupid:

> One of the very first requirements for a man who is fit to handle pig iron as a regular occupation is that he shall be so stupid . . . that he more nearly resembles in his mental make-up the ox than any other type.[5]

This also implied that workers were usually unable to determine how they could best do their jobs, leading to a further loss of productivity.

Both issues were addressed by his system of scientific management. The laziness issue was resolved by devising intricate piece-rate systems, such that workers who worked hard and achieved a particular minimum output were paid according to higher rates than others, thus providing workers with a strong incentive to work hard. According to Taylor, this resulted in both higher productivity and higher overall pay – at least for the highly productive "first-class" workers; others would typically end up earning less than before. The company management could address the stupidity issue by attending to four basic principles:

1 *Development of a true science*, that is, develop a "science" for each element of work. Tasks were examined closely by the management and its helpers and complex tasks were broken down into considerably smaller and simpler subtasks. The single best way of performing these tasks was determined by studying how the most productive workers did their jobs; other ways of doing this task were less productive and therefore suboptimal. In this way, tasks were broken down, simplified and stripped to their bare bones, devising a set of (very) simple tasks that could be performed in a fast and highly efficient manner. Further, these tasks and subtasks were timed with a stopwatch and the time needed for performing these tasks was established (a process known as "time study"), taking into account that workers needed frequent rest breaks (a novel insight at the time). This information was then used to establish the piece-rate system, giving an indication of how much output could reasonably be expected from a "fair day's work" and resulting in a high motivation to work hard. Further, in order to perform well, specialized tools for particular tasks were devised that would make it easier for workers to perform optimally.

2 *Scientific selection of the workman*. Before Taylor, workers were often hired on the basis of nepotism and favouritism, rather than whether they were fit for the job. Taylor insisted that foremen hire workers on the basis of their ability to do the job well, for example workers hired to handle pig iron should be physically strong as well as mentally sluggish; intelligent men would be

entirely unsuited to what would – for them – be the "grinding monotony of work of this character".

3 *Scientific education and development of workers.* After application of principles (1) and (2), management would have a set of standardized and scientifically optimized tasks at their disposal, would be aware of the single best way to conduct these tasks and would have hired a number of workers who should be well suited for these tasks. However, workers should still be familiarized with this one best way of doing their tasks. Since the tasks to be conducted were relatively simple, training the workers could be done quickly and cheaply, allowing them to conduct their tasks fast and efficiently.

4 And finally, there should be *intimate friendly cooperation between the management and the men.* Since "the workman who is best suited to actually doing the work is incapable of fully understanding this science", Taylor argued that there should be a far more equal division of responsibility between the workman and the management than was previously the case. Prior to Taylor, workers were held responsible for their performance and productivity. However, Taylor proposed that the management should take over much of the work now left to the men. In practice, this meant that the *planning* of the tasks (including establishing the "one best way" of doing the tasks, training workers as to how they should conduct their jobs, and deciding about the pay rates – all this was done by the management) was separated from their *execution* (which was reserved for the workers). In optimizing the production process, both parties should realize that their true interests were one and the same and that these interests were best served if of both parties cooperated together – labour unrest should be avoided, as this would in the long run be disadvantageous for both.

The reorganization of a company along the principles of scientific management would involve more than a new pay rate scheme and a scientific analysis of the tasks of workers. Most importantly, Taylor would also reform the management structure of the organization, especially focusing on the role of the mighty foremen. Before Taylor, foremen held many responsibilities, including running the production process, controlling the quality of the output, keeping cost records, hiring and firing of personnel, routing tasks to the machines and keeping track of the supplies. Obviously, being a foreman was a daunting job. Taylor would replace these *general* foremen with four *functional* foremen. The speed boss was responsible for driving the men, the gang-boss was in charge of tools and materials, an inspector checked the quality of the products and the repair boss made sure that the machinery was maintained well. Together they were responsible for the smooth and efficient operation of the production process. Moreover, he would instigate a planning department where the intellectual work – formerly also part of the tasks of the foreman – was done. This would include enforcing the piece rate, the flow of the production process, disciplining workers and the preparation of detailed instruction cards that would tell workers how to do their jobs. In spite of the fact that in this reform the ratio between "producers" (production workers) and "nonproducers" (all other staff) was worsened, it was intended to increase the efficiency of the production process. Further, by distributing the responsibilities, skills and knowledge of the general foreman across a larger number of functional foremen, the power of the general foreman as the single person responsible for running a particular department was broken; it was now up to the higher-level management to coordinate the activities of the functional foremen. In this way, a strong top-down structure for the management of the organization was created.

MATURATION OF THE SCIENTIFIC MANAGEMENT APPROACH

Taylor was eager to spread his ideas. He acted as a consultant for many organizations (both within and outside the US) and was seeing 40 to 50 people a week, all being interested in his methods. He read papers at the meetings of professional organizations such as the American Society of Mechanical Engineers. He published papers in various outlets and his main work (*The Principles of Scientific Management*, published in 1911) was soon translated in Chinese, Dutch, German, French, Italian and Russian. After his doctor advised him to restrict his working hours to 2.5 hours a day at maximum for health reasons, he continued to organize a weekly master class at Boxley. Here his guests (politicians, management researchers and consultants and business-people) were welcomed in the morning, receiving paper and pencil to make notes during the 2-hour lecture that would follow in the afternoon, in which Taylor would discuss the details of his system.[6] As for its content and delivery, a regular attendee of these meetings (Lillian Moller Gilbreth) noted that "Practically the same lecture seemed to be given each time . . . varying only in the illustrations chosen".[7] All this resulted in a set of devoted followers that formed the so-called Taylor Society in 1912 and that continued to meet after Taylor's death in 1915. In 1925, it had some 800 members, with many acting as management consultants (although that term was not yet in use) who propagated Taylor's ideas regarding the best way to organize an organization's production process.

Among the most notable and innovative members of the Taylor society were Lillian Moller Gilbreth and her husband, Frank Bunker Gilbreth. Frank Gilbreth had started as a bricklayer's apprentice in 1885 at age 17. After noting that veteran bricklayers each used motion in a different way and even before becoming aware of Taylor's work, he became interested in finding the best way of bricklaying. As Taylor would later appreciatively summarize, Gilbreth

decided to apply [the principles of scientific management] to the art of bricklaying. He . . . eliminated all unnecessary move-ments and substituted fast for slow motions. . . . He studied the best height for the mortar box and brick pile, and then designed a scaffold, with a table on it, upon which all of the materials are placed, so as to keep the bricks, the mortar, the man, and the wall in their proper relative positions. These scaffolds are adjusted, as the wall grows in height . . . Through all of this minute study. . . . Mr. Gilbreth has reduced his movements from eighteen motions per brick to five.

Evidently, this redesign of the task of bricklaying led to a great reduction of the time needed to complete projects. Gilbreth started his own successful contracting firm in 1895, the telling slogan of which was "speed work". He met Lillian Moller (a graduate from the University of California with a master in English literature and a strong interest in the emerging field of psychology) in 1903; the couple married a year later. Helped by the fact that the construction depression of the winter of 1911–1912 threatened his company to go into bankruptcy, Frank decided to pursue an alternative career in management consultancy; Lillian would become the systems manager in her husband's consulting firm. Together they became leaders in the new field of scientific industrial management, writing books and articles, lecturing and teaching.[8]

Lillian Gilbreth completed a dissertation in 1911 but was not awarded the degree due to noncompliance with residency requirements for doctoral candidates. It was published in 1914 as *The Psychology of Management* and was perhaps the first book to address the psychological aspects of scientific management. In this book, she presented her own views on this approach, building on the "recognition of the individual, not only as an economic unit but as a personality" and stressing the need to include the human element in management, including the effects of scientific management on the physical, mental and moral "welfare" of workers.[9] Moreover, Gilbreth's book discussed the *time-and-motion approach* which she developed together with her husband, extending Taylor's time study method with the possibilities offered by new technology. Whereas in Taylor's approach the actions of workers were timed using a stopwatch, the analysis of motions consisted in part of filming a worker's operations against a cross-sectioned background while a chronometer within the motion picture camera's field of vision counted time. In this way, a visual record was obtained that showed how work was done and how it could be improved. Moreover, by analyzing and comparing different ways of conducting a task they could synthesize the best elements of motion in these approaches to create a standardized best practice for the job. For example, the Gilbreths used this approach to conduct motion studies in surgery. The movements made by surgeons were analyzed to see if their work could be done more efficiently and therefore less fatiguing by eliminating unnecessary activities. One of their conclusions was that operating room nurses could improve efficiency. Surgeons spent more time on searching for their instruments when operating than on actually performing the operation. The Gilbreths therefore recommended that nurses should organize and lay out surgical instruments in regular and consistent patterns, to minimize the time needed for the surgeon to find the instruments to be used. The alignment of the work of physicians and nurses thus was (and still is) key to improving the efficiency of operating room processes.[10]

To Taylor, these extensions, innovations and improvements of his scientific management approach were largely wasted. Although he acknowledged the value of motion studies, he considered these as subordinate to his time study approach and certainly not as the major advance over time study publicized by Frank Gilbreth. The focus of the Gilbreths on the needs, personality and welfare (we would now say: health and well-being) of workers was lost on Taylor, who held on to his simplistic view of worker motivation as being solely a matter of pay. In turn, the Gilbreths were convinced that the successful implementation of Taylor's ideas would require hard work by both engineers and psychologists, and that Taylor's version of scientific management fell short when it came to managing the human element on the shop floor.[11] In 1914 the Gilbreths broke with Taylor, after Frank handled a contract with the New Jersey-based Herrman-Aukam company (a producer of handkerchiefs) to the dissatisfaction of its owners. They approached Taylor with complaints about the pace and quality of Gilbreth's work, after which Taylor recommended one of his more orthodox disciples to finish Gilbreth's job.

After the breach with Taylor, the Gilbreths continued to form and enthusiastically marketed their own version of scientific management as being more concerned with the human factor. Lillian completed her PhD in psychology in 1915 and Frank strongly relied on her in doing the intellectual work associated with spreading the couple's ideas. Importantly, this took the form of a series of articles in which Lillian argued that motion study aimed to accurately determine the fatigue resulting from any job, eliminating that what was unnecessary by designing convenient work benches, furnishing chairs, providing opportunities for rest and recovery and so on. In this way, motion study not only enhanced efficiency but also was presented as having tangible benefits for workers in reducing levels of fatigue. Moreover, by performing a fatigue survey on first entering a factory, by providing quick fixes for fatigue-producing activities such as standing and stretching and by holding open meetings to discuss the progress of the reorganization process, the chance of acceptance of scientific management techniques (including motion study) on the shop floor was further enhanced.

When Frank died unexpectedly in 1924, Lillian kept up the family business, advising the Hoover, Eisenhower and Truman administrations during the 1930s through the 1950s and obtaining a tenured position as the first female professor (of Management) at Purdue University in 1935, where she focused on the optimal design of workplaces and kitchens. She was instrumental in designing the L and U-shaped kitchen layouts used today, in which the idea is to create a tight circuit for the cook, with no or only little need to move the feet. She is also credited with the invention of the foot pedal trash can and the shelves on the inside of refrigerator doors (including the indispensable egg keeper), she filed patents involving improvements on household appliances such as the electric can opener and she is considered the founder of both the fields of ergonomics and management. After a busy life – next to the family business, the Gilbreths had 12 children – she retired in 1968 at age 89, passing away in 1972.

CRITICISMS OF SCIENTIFIC MANAGEMENT

Scientific management has frequently been criticized on various grounds. One class of criticisms refers to *moral/political* issues. By simplifying work tasks, the workers on the factory floor experienced a huge loss in dignity, skills and power. In a sense, Taylor's reforms would take away knowledge (and, thus, power) away from the worker, transferring it to management, meaning that where formerly (well-paid) skilled workers were needed, now (much cheaper and easily replaceable) unskilled workers could be trained to do their jobs, which obviously did little for the bargaining position of workers.

A second class of criticism refers to the fact that Taylorized work (i.e. simplified, repetitive, effort-intensive, low-skills, low-brains and low-freedom work) was not particularly motivating for workers. Basically, this is Marx and Engels' criticism that Taylorized work "has lost all individual character, and, consequently, all charm for the workman". This is difficult to deny, but to his defence, Taylor never claimed that under scientific management work would be more challenging and more fun for the worker, only that it would pay better.

Third, Taylorism has been criticized on the grounds that application of its principles would not have the positive consequences that it was supposed to have. For instance, in his magnum opus *The Principles of Scientific Management*, Taylor greatly exaggerated the positive effects of scientific management on productivity and efficiency, to the degree that the applications presented there were closer to fiction than to fact.[12] However, whereas these specific examples may not hold water, many applications of the principles of scientific management were certainly successful, leading to their wide adoption. In this sense, the fact that Taylor fabricated part of the evidence supporting his ideas is irrelevant for the value of his approach.

Finally, the principles of scientific management might seem outdated today. Taylor and his associates developed their ideas more than a century ago, when blue-collar jobs (involving physically demanding manual labour such as shovelling or bricklaying) were common. Conversely, due to economic and technological developments such as the ever-increasing use of ICT, many of us hold neat white-collar (professional, managerial or administrative work in an office) or pink-collar (service-oriented work, related to customer interaction, entertainment or sales work) jobs. Are the principles of scientific management also relevant to today's professions?

Certainly there are major differences between the jobs for which scientific management was initially developed and the jobs in our society. However, this does not mean that the principles of scientific management do not apply to these occupations. On the one hand, in their generalized form the central notions of scientific management are very much alive and well today and can be recognized in nearly all work contexts. These ideas include a strong fascination for productivity and efficiency; the use of systematic analysis to determine the best methods and procedures for conducting tasks; the selection, training and development of workers using scientifically proven methods; the development of standardized procedures and tools; the setting of specific tasks and goals; the idea that workers and management have mutual interests and should cooperate in optimizing the production process; and rewarding employees using pre-specified incentive schemes if they achieve these goals.[13] Indeed, one may argue that these ideas are by now so well accepted and widely used that we tend to take them for granted; it is difficult to see how (and perhaps even why) things should be arranged differently. The distinction between planning and doing has received more criticism, leading to the development of various alternative approaches (see Chapters 3 and 4). But even so, this principle is often clearly visible in current organizations where responsibilities and opportunities for decision making tend to be separated hierarchically, although not always as rigorously and systematically as proposed by Taylor.

On the other hand, the introduction of new technology has sharpened the split between thinking and doing even further. Work is more and more divided in two streams: skilled programming, planning and analytical work at the top and low-skilled program execution at the bottom, increasing the degree to which those at the bottom function as (and often feel like) cogs in a big machine. There is no doubt that Taylor and his disciples would have loved (and used) the possibilities for simplifying tasks and increasing control offered by ICT – not only to manage workers in blue-collar jobs, but certainly also those holding white- and pink-collar jobs.[14] In this sense, modern technology has helped and will certainly continue to help bring about a society that is to an increasing degree organized on the basis of the principles of scientific management.

EFFECTIVENESS OF SCIENTIFIC MANAGEMENT

The rationalization of working life that started with the advent of the industrial revolution is an ongoing process, and to date it has by no means been completed. Taylor, the Gilbreths and others did not initiate these developments, and their efforts coincided with or were followed by many other developments, including the famous introduction of conveyor belt assembly lines in 1913 by Henry Ford. That is, mass production of products was made possible by combining the principles of scientific management (with its focus on routinizing, standardizing and simplifying labour) with the idea that products can be standardized as well, allowing for the production of large numbers of goods and products at low costs.

Yet Taylor and this associates were among the very first to think systematically about the best way to organize labour in the industrial era, using, explicating, generating and combining insights offered by technology and the then-emerging disciplines of organizational science, ergonomics and industrial psychology to create work environments that were expected to benefit organizations and workers as well as society as a whole. Essentially, their efforts were directed towards making workers work harder and faster to achieve better performance, resulting in stronger organizations that can compete more efficiently (and, hence, more successfully) with their competitors. Clearly, their ideas have exerted a major influence on the way we currently work – they still do, and they can easily be recognized in many aspects of current working life.

But were their ideas effective in making workers more productive? Stated in such general terms, this question is difficult and perhaps even uninteresting to answer. Some of the principles prescribed by Taylor (e.g. that the interests of workers and management are actually the same) can best be considered political axioms with which one may agree or disagree, rather than as testable hypotheses. Other ideas seem so obvious that rigid empirical research is superfluous. For example, it goes without saying that tasks are often conducted best using tools that are well designed for the job, that surgeons can perform more efficiently if their surgical instruments are kept well organized and that it is efficient to search for best practices if a task can be conducted in more than a single way. Finally, the experiments conducted by Taylor, the Gilbreths and others are considered inconclusive at best due to all sorts of fallacies and fabrications;[11] they would not be informative for the design of today's jobs anyway.

However, over the last decades, much knowledge has been generated that is relevant to evaluating parts of the principles of scientific management. For example, Taylor proposed that workmen should be scientifically selected and trained for the job, leading to the creation of what would later become known as the human resource departments in organizations. But does a careful *selection of workers* in terms of their personality, intelligence and skills lead to improved worker performance, or is this mainly a sort of ritual dance that has no measurable effects on performance? This is the topic of Chapter 5. Taylor (and later Lillian Gilbreth) are credited with the idea that work should contain sufficient opportunity for *rest and recovery* – however, are work performance and worker well-being actually enhanced by introducing breaks at work (Chapter 6)? Before turning to these and other issues, the next chapters address Taylor's key assumption that working conditions (including among others *incentive schemes* and the degree to which *planning and doing are separated* in a job) affect worker motivation, well-being and performance.

3

IT'S LIFE, JIM, LIFE AS WE KNOW IT

Happiness at work

A wintery Monday morning in Cicero, Illinois, 1926. The windows of the room in the giant Hawthorne plant of Western Electric Company are taped black in order to keep the daylight out. The girls coming in for work notice something odd about the lighting in the room. The light bulbs have been replaced during the weekend, now producing the equivalent of the light of a couple of lit candles. The girls have work to do: winding small induction coils on wooden spools for use in telephone switchboards. But due to the bad lighting conditions, the women are complaining, saying that they are hardly able to see what they are doing.[1] Why would the company management attempt to hinder its employees in performing well?

TOWARDS A PSYCHOLOGICAL APPROACH OF PROMOTING WORKER PRODUCTIVITY

In the 1900–1920s, organizations became more and more interested in ways to improve worker productivity. The ideas promoted by Frederick Taylor and his disciplines caught on, both nationally and internationally, and companies were frantically seeking for ways to increase their output, competitiveness and, ultimately, their profitability. Research on productivity was made possible through partnerships among industries, universities and government. Initiated by the National Research Council, in the 1920s and early 1930s, the Western Electric Company conducted a series of classic behavioural experiments in which the effects of working conditions such as lighting, wage incentives, rest pauses and working hours on worker productivity were studied. The results of these experiments – now collectively known as the *Hawthorne studies* – are interesting and have been much debated up to the present day, for two reasons.

First, the findings of the Hawthorne studies are now widely considered inconclusive. For example, the common belief that the *illumination experiments* referred to earlier showed that productivity increased, independent of the level of lighting, has been discredited by a re-analysis of the original data.[2] In the series of experiments that started in 1927 in the so-called *relay assembly room*, conditions of work were changed one at a time: rest periods of different numbers and lengths, the working day was shortened and wage incentives were given. Interestingly, with each subsequent change, productivity rose. However, when in the 12th week of the experiment the working conditions were reversed to their original levels, productivity continued to increase as well. Elton Mayo, the academic leader of the programme, decided that this was due to the fact that during the experiment, workers had been consulted with respect to the proposed changes: they

> had arrived at the point of free expression of ideas and feelings to the management . . . the six individuals became a team and the team gave itself wholeheartedly and spontaneously to co-operation in an experiment.[3]

Mayo felt that the manipulations of the working conditions were relatively unimportant: it was the social context that mattered. Mental attitudes, proper supervision, informal social relationships experienced in a group and worker involvement in the decisions taken at work were key to productivity and job satisfaction. Critics have pointed out that this conclusion was not warranted by the data and that the rising productivity levels could be due to a host of other factors, including the fact that two of the women who were initially included in the experiment were replaced halfway with more productive colleagues, because they had become "antagonistic" and had "turned Bolshevik". Mayo's statement that "the team gave itself wholeheartedly and spontaneously to co-operation" evidently required a good deal of re-interpretation of the data. It is clear that the Hawthorne experiments do not meet current standards and that their main conclusion – that productivity at work is not only (and not even mainly) a consequence of the sort of intricate incentive schemes devised by the likes of Frederick Taylor, but that social factors are at least as important – is not warranted.

Second, and perhaps more important, the Hawthorne experiments have profoundly transformed the way we look at workers and the organizations they work for. Their premises, approaches used and conclusions may have been false, but even faulty insights and beliefs can be very real in their consequences. In the case of the Hawthorne studies, this research bolstered what is now known as the *human relations movement*, has strongly influenced the relations between employees and their employers, and was the start of the modern academic discipline of organizational behaviour/industrial psychology. In this sense, these experiments have instigated a major shift away from simplistic Tayloristic thinking about the best way to increase organizational productivity, towards more social-psychological approaches to promoting worker productivity. It has therefore been argued that the value of the Hawthorne studies does not lie in their findings. Rather, their value lies in the fact that this research generated new ideas, questions and hypotheses on the relationships between work motivation, supervision, social relations and decision making at work in general, and on the association between job satisfaction on the one hand and performance on the other in particular.[4]

Of course, generating theoretically interesting questions is fine, but has the research that has been conducted since the 1930s also generated practically useful *answers* as to how to workers can be motivated, how their productivity can be promoted and the like?

DOES PROVIDING FINANCIAL INCENTIVES ENHANCE WORK PERFORMANCE?

The idea that workers will work harder and be more productive if they are motivated with proper incentives goes a long way back. According to Frederick Taylor, one of the most important steps to be taken in raising worker productivity was the introduction of a piece-rate system, in which workers would receive a progressively higher rate of pay with increasing output. Working twice as hard would thus result in more than double the pay, providing workers with a strong incentive to increase the effort they invested in their jobs. The idea behind these strategies is that money speaks louder than words: by rewarding employees on the basis of their results (and not, or not solely, on the basis of the amount of time they spend on their jobs), companies can keep their employees on their toes.

According to its proponents, the introduction of a piece-rate pay system will have at least three advantages for the organization. First, since workers are being paid on the basis of their output, not working efficiently and quickly will directly translate into income losses. They will therefore work hard, even in the absence of constant supervision. Second, workers will be motivated to find innovative and more efficient ways to do the job, beyond the "one best way" dictated by the employer. Workers will thus produce and earn more, while the organization profits from not only their higher productivity but also their creativity in developing better ways to conduct their tasks. Third, since workers will be more productive, the number of products finished will be larger. This will lead to advantages of scale and a further increased efficiency (and profits!) for the organization, for example fixed overhead costs (such as factory rent and insurance costs) can then be written off across a larger number of products, meaning that their price will drop and that their sales will increase. From an economic point of view this is good for customers, society and the organization alike (environmentalists are welcome to disagree, of course).

Consistent with this reasoning, the scientific literature is abundant with experiments, case-studies and anecdotal evidence showing that the introduction of piece-rate pay systems in organizations is associated with higher worker productivity. Other accounts show that productivity may become higher but that this does not necessarily imply that organizational profits and efficiency increase as well. Yet other research reports no statistically significant relationship between the introduction of piece-rate systems and performance. In order to make sense of this scattered and sometimes conflicting evidence, researchers in this area have conducted reviews and meta-analyses in which they discuss and integrate the findings of an usually large number of previous empirical studies on the issue of interest. The advantage of such approaches is that, rather than to focus on the details of single studies, they provide a robust overall impression of the findings concerning a particular issue.

For example, a review study involving 39 studies on the association between the provision of financial incentives on the one hand and performance quantity (i.e. output) on the other found that providing financial incentives was indeed associated with higher performance.[5] This study showed that the way of rewarding workers (providing or not providing them with incentives for their performance) accounted for roughly 11 per cent of the differences in their performance. Focusing on field studies only (i.e. studies conducted in real-life settings, not studies conducted in university labs or experimental simulation studies), this figure increased to 21 per cent. Although this may seem rather modest (after all, 79 per cent of the individual variation in performance is not accounted for by the reward system), such an effect is surely relevant in today's globalized, heavy-competition world. This conclusion was substantiated by a more recent review study that focused exclusively on field studies in which the reward system was either changed (e.g. from piece rates to a flat hourly pay rate or vice versa). Basically, this study concluded that "if you reward workers for their output, they produce".[6]

THE DOWNSIDE OF PROVIDING FINANCIAL INCENTIVES

Overall, there can be little doubt that current evidence supports the idea that providing workers with financial incentives increases their productivity. Then why did piece-rate pay systems *decline* in the 20th century, at least in advanced economies?[7] Part of the answer probably lies in the fact that the piece-rate systems devised by Frederick Taylor and his colleagues were not only biased towards the interest of the employers, but were also widely considered harsh and inhuman, generating much opposition from workers and their representatives. Thus, labour unions attempted to introduce and retain remuneration systems that favour workers (i.e. time-based reward systems in which workers are paid on the basis of the number of hours spent on the job) rather than the organizations they work for. Another part of the answer may lie in the fact that much research on the effects of financial incentives has focused on simple tasks, relative to most jobs in the modern economy. For example, assembling an induction spool in the Hawthorne plant (an uncomplicated, repetitive and manual task) would take about one minute. If these assembly workers would work just a little bit harder, this could very well lead to readily-observable increases in the number of induction spools produced, for each worker separately. Compare this with the performance of, say, a kindergarten teacher, a middle manager or a nurse; how likely is it that their performance would improve if they were rewarded on the basis of a piece-rate system? Which aspect of their performance should be rewarded? And, in these cases, can performance be assigned unequivocally to individual workers, or are we talking about team-level performance? Obviously, designing a pay-for-performance incentive scheme that is suitable for today's jobs is no easy feat. Moreover, it seems that the implementation of incentive-based pay systems may backfire, largely or even fully offsetting the presumed positive effects of such systems, for three broad classes of reasons.

First, a major drawback of providing workers with financial incentives is that these may be *too* effective in directing employee behaviour. One line of reasoning here is that there is a trade-off between quality and quantity: workers may devote their energy and skills to producing *many* products or to producing *high-quality* products, but they cannot do both. Thus, if incentives are given for producing many products, product quality may suffer. A related concern is that in their attempt to be efficient and productive, workers may focus exclusively on the tasks that are part of their formal job description (their in-role performance), neglecting anything going beyond these requirements. However, organizations usually function better if workers are also willing to perform tasks that go beyond their formal job prescription (i.e. extra-role performance), for instance, when they are also willing to help co-workers with a problem or to maintain a pleasurable work climate (e.g. by helping organize the yearly organizational outing).[8] Again, in the absence of a sizeable body of relevant research, it is difficult to say whether this reasoning holds water. A third concern here is that providing workers with financial incentives may lead them to attempt to game the system, that is, workers may use the rules and procedures of the remuneration system to manipulate this system for a desired outcome – usually higher pay or faster promotion. For example, derivatives broker Nick Leeson was responsible for the collapse of Barings bank in 1995 due to unauthorized, highly speculative trading. In 1992, this resulted in a £130,000 bonus on top of his already comfortable £50,000 salary for that year. Unfortunately, his luck soon turned sour, in 1995 resulting in an £827 million loss for his employer. Barings was subsequently declared insolvent. In the subsequent decade, the global financial crisis of the late 2000s resulted at least partly from "predatory lending practices", in which unscrupulous banks enticed borrowers to enter high-risk loans for short-term profit. These examples show that providing workers with incentives for particular behaviours will lead them to engage in the desired behaviours – but possibly at the cost of other desirable behaviours.

Second, finding and fixing on a reasonable pay rate is often a daunting task, especially if piece rates are adjusted downwards. Workers and their representatives will be motivated to set the rate so high as to allow workers to earn a decent wage without overly exhausting themselves. Conversely, employers will attempt to set the rate as low as possible, increasing the pressure on their employees to work hard. Chances are that the parties involved in a bargaining process over the right pay rate will find that (in Frederick Taylor's terms) there is no "friendly cooperation between the management and the men" here, as their "true interests" will differ too strongly.[9]

Finally, piece-rate systems will put high pressure on employees to work hard, with possibly adverse consequences for their health and well-being. On the one hand, being paid on a piece-rate basis could lead to higher levels of worker stress, fatigue and the like, affecting their health and well-being negatively. In Chapter 6, we discuss the delicate balance between work effort and recovery from that effort in more detail. On the other hand, the adverse effects of piece-rate systems on employee health and well-being could be due to a possible trade-off between productivity and safety. If workers are paid on the basis of their productivity, they may focus on producing many and/or high-quality products rather than on attending to time-consuming health and safety regulations. For example, truck drivers on a piece-rate system may drive faster than is allowed or may neglect taking breaks in order to get their freight faster to their clients. This may lead them to drive while fatigued, which will in turn lead to higher accident rates, also affecting others than the truck driver himself or herself. A review of 31 studies on the association between piece rates and worker health and safety showed that no fewer than 27 of these reported negative effects of piece rates on safety behaviour, leading the authors to conclude that "in most situations piece rates have negative effects on health and safety".[10]

Overall, whereas it is clear that providing workers with financial incentives for particular behaviours will often result in higher productivity, it is equally clear that doing so may not always (or not only) have the effects desired by the organization. There may be ways to realize the benefits of providing incentives on worker performance without experiencing its disadvantages. For example, a worker's pay may to an only limited degree be dependent on his or her productivity, for example by providing workers with a bonus for good performance on top of a fixed hourly pay rate if they perform exceptionally well. However, the Nick Leeson case discussed earlier shows that the combination of a fixed wage and overly large bonuses can still induce counterproductive behaviours.

The available evidence suggests that using financial incentives for improving work performance can be attractive to organizations when four conditions are met. First, the tasks to be conducted should be relatively simple, and it should be difficult for these tasks to be done badly (there should be no trade-off between quantity and quality). Second, adverse effects should be unlikely to occur, and if they occur, they should not have overly serious consequences (such as the demise of the organization or even a world-wide financial crisis). Third, it should be clear which behaviours are rewarded, and it should be possible to measure these behaviours individually. And finally, the organization, unions or workers should not care much about issues like stress, quality of employment, safety at work and worker health and well-being. Although this fourth condition may frequently have been met in the 19th century, nowadays this is very different, and perhaps rightly so. Indeed, the Hawthorne experiments have made organizations, workers and the general public aware of the fact that work motivation and productivity are not just a matter of providing workers with the right financial incentives. They have led to the discovery of the worker as a human being with similar needs, wants and desires as the managers and owners for which they worked. In a sense, Elton Mayo's (1945) book on the Hawthorne experiments can be read as a *Star Trek* scenario in which, after much experimentation and not-so-scientific analysis, the main character – a Spock-eared management consultant perhaps – concludes that the odd creatures down in the production department are "life, Jim, life as we know it".

HAPPY WORKERS, PRODUCTIVE WORKERS?

A considerable body of research has addressed the idea that work motivation as a major antecedent of work performance can be increased by focusing on other factors than financial incentives only; factors that tap into the human needs to feel valued, in control and competent, to have meaningful social interactions at work, and to feel satisfied with and, well, *happy* about their job. This belief – that is currently widely held by managers, employees and laymen alike – is commonly referred to as the *happy-productive worker hypothesis* and dates back to at least the 1930s. For example, in 1932, an in-depth qualitative study conducted by Wharton professor Rexford B. Hersey found that the productivity of happy workers was increased in 30 to 40 per cent of the time, decreased in 10 per cent and unchanged in the remaining instances. Moreover, emotions (e.g. "irritable", "angry", "elated" and "cheerful") were the most important concomitants of productivity changes. Upon inspection of the patterns of emotions reported by his subjects, Hersey found that these followed a cycle of 5 to 6 weeks, arguing that knowledge of one's emotional rhythms would help people to predict the days on which they were most likely to succeed. The evidence on these emotional cycles is even more remarkable when taking into account that all participants in these experiments were male.[11]

This somewhat anecdotal evidence for an association between worker happiness and productivity was confirmed by a major review study incorporating 312 independent samples, comprising more than 54,000 participants. This study showed that individual differences in general job satisfaction accounted for about 9 per cent of the differences in in-role job performance, with satisfied, "happy" workers performing better than others.[12] However, all studies included in this review were non-experimental, and in most of these the presumed cause (satisfaction) and outcome (performance) were measured at the same point in time. Correlation is not causation, and without information about the temporal order in which these concepts occurred, we do not know what is the "cause" and what the "effect" here. Perhaps satisfaction does indeed cause performance. But these findings could also mean that performance causes satisfaction, or that satisfaction and performance mutually affect each other. One way out of this problem is to focus on studies in which the participants are followed across time, taking multiple measures of the presumed cause (satisfaction) and outcome (performance). Unfortunately, a review of 14 longitudinal studies provided no compelling evidence for the idea that satisfaction causes performance. Although overall the effect of job satisfaction on later job performance was slightly stronger than the reverse effect, it was so small that practical implications were largely absent.[13]

Do these findings mean that people are mistaken in believing that happy workers are likely to be more productive than others? Hardly so. Longitudinal studies are beset with problems, one of which being that we do not know how the causal processes linking two concepts unfold across time. Sometimes such processes take a very long time. For instance, the adverse effects of being exposed to asbestos on health can be detected only in studies covering very long time periods – 10 years or more. No effects will be detected in studies covering only a couple of weeks, because the diseases associated with exposure to asbestos (mainly various types of cancer) need considerably more time to manifest itself. Other processes develop relatively quickly and can be studied well only in studies covering relatively short periods. Interestingly, in the review study cited earlier, the across-time effects of job satisfaction on performance were stronger for short study periods (covering 1 to 6 months) than for longer periods, suggesting that the positive effects of high satisfaction on performance are short lived. This would seem intuitively plausible, in that both satisfaction and performance could vary substantially across time. As indicated earlier, Professor Hersey already found apparently meaningful variation in both concepts for a 1-month interval, and a more recent review reported that the associations between happiness and performance were especially strong when both concepts referred to the same *day*, rather than to a longer period.[14] Consequently, it seems fair to conclude that (a) job satisfaction and job performance are positively related, (b) this association is considerably stronger on the short run than on the long run and (c) there is evidence that this relationship can be interpreted causally, in line with the happy-productive worker hypothesis.

BURNOUT, ENGAGEMENT AND PRODUCTIVITY

The happy-productive worker hypothesis has been tested with not only job satisfaction as an indicator of worker happiness. One important indicator of the *absence* of worker happiness is burnout. This concept was introduced in 1974 by Herbert Freudenberger, who used the term to describe the gradual emotional depletion, reduced commitment and loss of motivation among the volunteers working with the homeless people and drug addicts of the St Mark's Free Clinic in New York's East Village that Freudenberger observed as a consulting psychiatrist. Freudenberger knew what he was talking about: he himself fell victim to burnout twice. Independently and simultaneously, Christina Maslach and her colleagues came across the term when conducting a study among human services workers. When interviewing her participants, she found that these workers often felt emotionally exhausted and depleted of energy, reported negative attitudes towards their clients or patients and were doubting their professional competence – a syndrome to which these workers referred as "burnout".[15] Maslach and her colleagues later developed the Maslach Burnout Inventory (MBI) to tap these three aspects of burnout, labelling these "exhaustion", "cynicism" and "reduced personal accomplishment", respectively. Although other instruments are available, the MBI has become the gold standard when studying burnout.

High scores on burnout have been linked to high levels of physical and mental complaints (such as depression), sickness absence, turnover and low commitment to the organization. Perhaps not surprisingly, as a strong indicator of the absence of worker happiness it has also been related to low levels of performance. In a 24-study review, high levels of exhaustion, cynicism and low levels of personal accomplishment were all associated with on average lower scores on performance, accounting for 4 to 12 per cent of the individual variation in self-reported performance.[16] Another review focused exclusively on non-self-reported performance (e.g. as reported by the worker's colleagues, supervisor or clients; sales; or the number of products delivered), finding that especially high levels of exhaustion were associated with lower performance, accounting for 4 per cent to as much as 30 per cent of the individual differences in performance.[17]

A second often-studied indicator of worker happiness is work engagement. Although the exact origin of the term is unknown, at present, work engagement is often considered the positive antithesis of burnout. Burned-out workers suffer from exhaustion, are cynical about their job and feel insecure about their performance. Conversely, engagement is characterized by high levels of energy, involvement and efficacy, respectively – the opposite of the three dimensions of burnout. Not surprisingly, burnout and engagement tend to be moderately strongly related. It can therefore be expected that engagement relates to work performance as well. Consistent with this reasoning, three researchers from the Spanish universities of Castellón and Valencia conducted a study using data from 58 hotel receptions and 56 restaurants. For each of these, three employees and ten customers completed a questionnaire. Consistent with the happy-productive worker hypothesis, the results showed that the customers of restaurants and receptions with engaged, "happy" staff were considerably more satisfied with their services than clients of other restaurants and hotels.[18] A similar study involving nearly 8,000 business units of 36 US companies in the financial, manufacturing, services, retail and transportation sectors confirmed that high-engagement business units were evaluated more positively by their customers, had better safety records and were more productive and profitable than other units. What is interesting about this study is that the effects of job satisfaction and engagement on performance could be compared, showing that both concepts accounted for about 14 per cent of the differences in business-unit performance.[19] Thus, work engagement and burnout are both relevant as possible antecedents of work performance.

FINANCIAL INCENTIVES, HAPPINESS AND PERFORMANCE

Frederick Taylor did not care much about the health and well-being of workers. If being unproductive on the job and earning little in the process made workers happy, fine – that was their choice. He was convinced that his scientific management approach would ultimately make workers happier, but this would be due to receiving a higher pay (courtesy of his cutting-edge remuneration schemes) and the ability to buy more and better products, rather than to being happy on the job itself. The evidence discussed in this chapter suggests that focusing on piece rates and pay-for-performance can indeed be effective in motivating workers to give their best – sometimes even too effective, as such incentives will lead workers to focus exclusively on the type of behaviours that maximize the incentives to be received. As we have seen, this may not always be in the best interest of the worker, the organization they work for or society as a whole.

The ideas of Elton Mayo and the likes were radically different. In their interpretation of the Hawthorne experiments, these had shown that features other than remuneration and physical working conditions were essential in improving worker productivity. Especially the human aspects of work – the relationships with one's fellow workers and supervisor – were considered important in improving worker motivation. Basically, they argued that management should treat workers as individuals, each with their own needs, and that doing so would lead workers to be satisfied. In turn, this would increase their willingness to cooperate with management, contributing their efforts towards accomplishing organizational goals. Again, the evidence that is currently available is in line with these ideas – happy, satisfied, engaged and not-burned-out workers tend to perform better than others.

Thus, it appears that work performance can be promoted in both ways. But is there *one best way* in motivating workers to work hard? Unfortunately, comparative research on the effects of promoting worker happiness versus providing financial incentives is absent, meaning that this question cannot easily be answered. Psychologists are not economists, and rigid evaluations of the costs versus the returns of interventions for promoting worker happiness are absent. However, there is some evidence that paying attention to workplace safety does pay off. For example, a 2012 study showed that inspections of California's Division of Occupational Safety and Health resulted in a 9.4 per cent drop in injury claims and saved the inspected firms on average 26 per cent ($355,000) in injury claims and compensation paid for lost work over the 4 years after an inspection, compared to similar uninspected workplaces.[20] Similarly, since happy workers tend to leave organizations less often than other workers (saving organizations the costs of hiring and training new workers) and are less frequently ill and absent than others, it can be assumed that investments in worker happiness will reap at least some financial return. However, although the European Agency for Safety and Health at Work cheerfully says that "very cheap investments in occupational safety and health often create large returns", it also cautions that "investment in occupational safety and health is not always beneficial. Like any other type of investment, it might be economically profitable or not".[21]

It may be concluded that whereas there may be a business case for investments in worker health and well-being, it is perhaps not as strong and convincing as would be desirable. However, investing in happiness is not a cheap alternative to giving employees a raise, and financial gain is not the only reason why organizations should invest in worker well-being. National and international law specifies that it is an employer's duty to provide its employees with safe and healthy workplaces. Thus, employers may well believe that incentives work best, but they must still invest in the safety and well-being of their employees. And if this fails to convince them, there is always the issue of human decency: even simple, low-skills and repetitive production work is done by people like us, *life as we know it*. For which reasons would *you* like to work hard? Because your job is challenging, pleasurable and even fun, or only because at the end of the day you bring in a couple of dollars?

But let's look at this issue from the bright side. The present chapter showed that current evidence supports the idea that happy workers are more productive than others. An important corollary of this conclusion is that enhancing worker productivity does not need to come at the cost of worker happiness: by focusing on the latter, both can be promoted simultaneously. Therefore, a central question is: how can organizations improve the health and well-being (the *happiness*) of their employees?

4

PROMOTING HAPPINESS AT WORK

Former US president Ronald Reagan – a Republican – once said, "The nine most terrifying words in the English language are, I'm from the government and I'm here to help". Nine other words are perhaps not that frightening, but some of you may feel that they are equally bizarre: *As your employer, I want to make you happy*. Why would an organization care about the happiness of its employees? That can't be good – surely there is some hidden agenda here!

MODELS FOR WORKER HAPPINESS

As discussed in Chapter 3, employers have good reason to attempt to influence the health, well-being and even happiness of their employees: having happy, satisfied, engaged and non-burned out employees is good for business (not much of a hidden agenda here), an idea dating back to at least the human relations movement of the 1930s. It is therefore important for us to understand what makes people happy at work: which features of their jobs make them feel good about their jobs and fire their enthusiasm, motivation and work performance?

In the past five decades or so, this issue has sparked much interest among organizational researchers. To this aim, they have devised so-called *models* for the relations between certain sets of job characteristics and all sorts of "work outcomes". Essentially, a model is a simplified representation of a part of reality, focusing on the features of that reality that are considered most relevant for the author's purpose. For example, the London Underground map shows how the stations of the underground are connected. It is not a geographically correct representation of the centre of London, and it does not contain details on its streets, rivers and lakes, parks, railways, towns, et cetera. If these concern you or if you would need to find a specific address (say, 221b Baker Street), a regular London map will be much more useful. In some occasions, a simplified tourist map showing only its main streets and attractions may suit you even better. These three types of maps constitute different models of London, designed for different purposes and focusing on different parts of reality. Importantly, models are not just representations of reality – they also predict what will happen, given that the model's assumptions are satisfied. If you board the Victoria line at Walthamstow Central, you will get to Pimlico in about 40 minutes, assuming that there are no delays or closures. There is no absolute certainty that the Victoria will take you there in 40 minutes, but under normal circumstances, boarding this line is your best bet of getting there reasonably fast.

The work-psychological models discussed in this chapter are similar to maps. Their aim is to show how particular characteristics of a job (e.g. the variety it offers and the workload experienced by the workers having that job) relate to particular outcomes (such as productivity and well-being). Other characteristics and outcomes are not considered. Essentially, these models allow for statements like, "If you want to arrive at highly productive workers, your best bet is to focus on improving job characteristic x or y". That is, these models assume that the job characteristics included in these models causally affect work outcomes such as job satisfaction, productivity and well-being: do this, and that will usually be the result.

As an example, take a factory worker who assembles small electronic parts to be used in cell telephones. Work pressure is high, as the assembly line is running fast. Talking to colleagues is difficult as they, too, are working hard. There is little variety as to the tasks themselves;

the worker produces the same parts all day long. Decisions regarding the speed of working, working times, breaks, et cetera, are taken by a supervisor. Promotion opportunities are largely absent, and pay is bad. The parts are produced for use in phones, but as these are assembled elsewhere, the worker does not even know which phone is being produced. This company's management may want to know, how can the productivity and/or well-being of this worker be improved? The models presented in this chapter attempt to answer this question. Some state that your best bet would be to improve pay, others state that workers should be given more freedom in deciding about their work and working times and yet other models propose that the variety offered by the job should be enlarged, et cetera.

In a sense, these models are different maps of the same geographical area, and it is up to the user to decide which map (model) is best suited for his or her purposes. But in order to identify that model, it is helpful to have a rough understanding of what these models actually involve: what are the alternatives to model x or y? Therefore, in the following we focus on the main features of and findings obtained for the most important models for the relations between work characteristics and work outcomes. Importantly, the insights generated by these models are by no means only interesting from a scientific point of view. They also generate practically important insights on the way that jobs should be *designed*. That is, all models are designed to see how the work can be shaped to improve well-being and also to increase performance, providing practical guidance as to how particular desired outcomes can be brought about.

THE JOB CHARACTERISTICS MODEL

Against the backdrop of stable employment and mass manufacture of the 1960s and 1970s in advanced Western economies, professors Richard Hackman from Harvard and Greg Oldham from the University of Illinois developed their *Job Characteristics Model* (JCM), which was the first "modern classic" of job design.[1] Their model proposes that five core job dimensions affect three critical psychological states, which in turn lead to a range of personal and job outcomes. These core job dimensions are:

- *Skill variety*: a call centre worker taking calls from customers all day has less skill variety than a carpenter who designs and produces custom-made furniture, using a wide range of tools, skills and techniques.
- *Task identity* refers to the extent to which workers do a complete (from beginning to end) and identifiable, visible piece of work, as opposed to doing only part of the work. For example, a writer working on a book has high task identity; workers producing small parts for use in cell phones have low task identity.
- *Task significance* refers to the degree to which jobs impact upon others. A country's Prime Minister will likely experience more task significance than the driver of his or her official state car.
- A high degree of *autonomy* means that workers have much freedom in deciding what they do, and when, where and how they execute their tasks. For example, the autonomy (and creativity) of designers of cheap furniture is often restricted by the fact that they cannot use expensive materials or complicated designs. Think of products like IKEA's practical but plain Billy bookcase system, to be assembled by customers using only an Allen key and a hammer and made of cheap foil and fibreboard. Conversely, when buyers complained about the comfort of his expensive red and blue chair (designed in 1917 and now in the permanent collection of New York's Museum of Modern Art), the celebrated Dutch designer Gerrit Rietveld retorted that "'to sit' is a verb" (i.e. not only an action in the grammatical sense, but also physically). Famous as he was, Rietveld even decided about how the product was to be evaluated: to him, comfort was irrelevant. Now *that* is autonomy!
- *Feedback from the job* pertains to the degree to which a job indicates how well the worker is performing. A computer programmer will immediately see whether or not his or her code produces the desired results. Conversely, a mayor who has implemented a

new crime reduction programme will see its results – if any – only after several years.

Hackman and Oldham proposed that a job's scores on skill variety, task identity and task significance should be averaged to provide an indication of the *experienced meaningfulness of the job*, one of three so-called critical psychological states. The second critical state is *experienced responsibility for work outcomes*, which is fully contingent on the autonomy offered by a job. Finally, the third psychological state – *knowledge of the results of work activities* – depends on the feedback obtained from the job. The multiplication of these three states yields the *motivational potential score* of the job. Adverse scores on the three critical psychological states are assumed to lead to low satisfaction, higher absence and turnover levels, and lower levels of job satisfaction, internal motivation and work effectiveness (performance). Further, the JCM also includes a personality characteristic, *growth need strength*, referring to the degree to which people have a need to develop and grow psychologically (e.g. by acquiring new skills). All workers will benefit from improvements in the five key factors of the JCM, but people with a high growth need are assumed to profit more.

In an early application of the model, 47 shop-floor employees in the production department of a confectionery factory in the north of England completed a questionnaire tapping most of the concepts listed earlier, plus mental health and performance. The number of absences and instances of being late were taken from the company's records. As expected, the five core job dimensions were related to the three critical psychological states, and these were in turn related to satisfaction and motivation. For the other outcomes, the results were inconclusive. Moreover, most of the relationships in this study were weak.[2] These mixed findings were replicated in an authoritative 200-study review study, concluding that the model received "modest" support. The associations among the five core job characteristics, the three psychological states and the personal and organizational outcomes were largely as predicted, but the effects of growth need strength varied with the type of outcome under consideration.[3]

These findings underline the idea that work characteristics are indeed important in affecting worker productivity and well-being. From a practical point of view, the JCM suggests that your best bet to improve worker productivity and well-being would be to increase skill variety, for example, by offering workers more opportunities to decide for themselves how to conduct a task – which tools, skills and techniques should be used? This will simultaneously increase worker autonomy. Perhaps it is possible to increase the degree to which workers can produce a complete piece of work rather than just its parts (task identity). Further, workers may be made aware of the importance of their contribution (task significance). And, finally, it is important for workers to receive information as to how well they are doing (feedback).

THE JOB DEMAND-CONTROL(-SUPPORT) MODEL

Since the 1990s, researchers (but not practitioners!) have turned away from the JCM, to models that – while often retaining some of its core ideas – considered other characteristics and that had other ideas concerning the relationships between work characteristics as antecedents of work outcomes. The most important of these is the Job Demand-Control(-Support) model.

In 1976, young Robert Karasek (already holding a BA in architecture and a MSc in civil engineering) submitted what would become one of the most influential PhD theses on the topic of work psychology ever, to the examination committee from the Massachusetts Institute of Technology.[4] When spending a year in Sweden on a Fulbright grant from the US State Department, he had become interested in "meaningful work experience", as it was expressed in connection with new town development outside Stockholm. At the time, it was feared that living in these suburbs would lead people to experience social isolation, alienation and apathy; would having a meaningful job affect these people positively, motivating them to become active in their communities? Incorporation of these new orientations to work seemed to imply major new challenges for thinking on work, work motivation and the outcomes thereof.

In his thesis, Karasek therefore attempted to integrate two different sets of outcomes that had been studied in different research traditions. In sociological approaches, the associations between social and psychological demands at work on the one hand and stress and illness on the other had been studied, without paying attention to the role of having control over these stressors. In contrast, the role of control at the workplace had been recognized in the job satisfaction literature (where task autonomy and skill variety were used as predictors of satisfaction, productivity and absenteeism, see Hackman and Oldham's JCM), but without considering the possible role of workload. Karasek integrated these perspectives in his *Job Demands-Control (JD-C) model*, arguing that the level of psychological demands would determine whether low levels of control would lead to either psychological strain or passive withdrawal. He defined *control* (or "decision latitude") as the combination of skill discretion (having a say over the skills and methods to be used on the job, relating to the repetitiveness and variety of the job) and decision authority (the ability to make decisions about one's job, to influence their work team and company policies in general). *Job demands* referred to the psychological stressors in the work environment, including time pressure, conflicting demands, degree of concentration required, pace of work and amount of work.

Karasek's model concentrates on two broad classes of outcomes: strain and health-related outcomes on the one hand, and activation/productivity-related outcomes on the other. The combination of control and demands leads to four types of jobs:

- High demands-low control (or *high strain*) jobs, leading to high levels of stress, strain and ill-health. For example, think of a waiter's job.
- High demands-high control (or *active*) jobs, in which the potentially adverse effects of having high demands are offset by the ability to decide how to respond optimally to the challenges of

the job. In such jobs, workers will thrive and even develop themselves, and will be productive and active (both on and off the job). For example, entrepreneurs often fall into this category.

- Low demands-low control (or *passive*) jobs, in which workers will experience little strain due to the absence of high demands. However, as they have little opportunity to exert control over their work situation, workers are likely to become passive and bored in the process, possibly even leading to the loss of skills. A typical example is the job of a watchman.
- Low demands-high control (relaxed, or *low strain*) jobs, in which workers will experience low levels of stress (few demands, lots of opportunities to experiment with new ways of dealing with these). Such idyllic jobs are rare, but tenured professors, carpenters and successful artists are sometimes mentioned as examples of jobs in this job category.

Later on, features of the social context (support experienced from co-workers and supervisor, including helping behaviours and informal talks) were added to the model (now labelled the *Job Demands-Control-Support, JDC-(S) model*); basically, the adverse effects of high demands and low control will be even stronger in the absence of support.[5]

To date, the JDC(-S) model has mainly been applied in the work context to study the effects of demands, control and support on worker well-being, strain and productivity. Apart from the focus on job demands as an additional antecedent of work outcomes, its most significant contribution is that it proposes that the adverse effects of high demands on work outcomes are mitigated in the presence of high levels of control. High control is expected to help workers dealing with the demands of their jobs, thus diminishing worker stress. Indeed, having high control could even turn high demands into challenges, increasing worker motivation to acquire new skills that will help them doing their job more efficiently and effectively. But do these attractive-sounding ideas hold water? Two review studies showed that high levels of control and support and low levels of demands were generally associated with better outcomes.[6,7] However, the idea that high control can somehow take away the bad effects of high demands received only limited support.

Practically, these findings mean that if worker health and well-being are to be improved, two obvious ways of doing so are to increase opportunities for control and social support. As regards the role of job demands, the evidence is mixed. Theoretically, optimal outcomes in terms of well-being and performance would be obtained when high demands are matched by high levels of control. However, in practice this reasoning does not hold; the best outcomes – at least in terms of well-being and health – are obtained when high scores on control and support coincide with low job demands. This may not sound like an overly attractive situation to organizations: "low demands"? Does that mean that my employees are slacking? There goes my profit! Please keep in mind that instruments measuring job demands tend to focus on rather extreme manifestations of high demands, such as having too little time for getting the job done, the need to do an excessive amount of work, or working very fast or hard. Thus, "low" scores on such instruments often mean that participants are productive, without feeling that their job is overtaxing them.

THE EFFORT-REWARD IMBALANCE MODEL

In a sense, workers must "invest" in their jobs: their time, skills, effort. They also expect to receive something in return: money, obviously, but also less tangible "rewards" such as esteem, a certain degree of job security and perhaps even good promotion prospects. Johannes Siegrist, a Swiss professor in medical sociology, took this reasoning as the starting point for his Effort-Reward Imbalance (ERI) model. Building on earlier notions that people seek equity in what they do, he proposed that workers strive to maintain a balance between their efforts and rewards at work. Effort refers to the demands of the job. This concept is similar to the concept of demands in Robert Karasek's JDC(-S) model but also involves obligations that are imposed on the employee, such as time pressure and working overtime. Occupational rewards are distributed by the employer and society at large: specifically money, esteem/approval and status control (referring to control over the continuity of one's role as a worker, that is, the degree of experienced job security and career opportunities). Workers will have no difficulties in accepting a situation in which their rewards exceed the effort they invest in their job. However, strong negative emotions such as stress and strain will occur if their effort exceeds the rewards they receive from that job. In turn, chronically high levels of chronic stress will ultimately have adverse consequences for health and well-being.[8]

Siegrist mentions three reasons why people would take or stay in a high effort-low rewards job. First, workers may have no choice but to accept this situation. For instance, alternative employment opportunities may be scarce due to personal or economic factors, such as being over 50 or an economic crisis. Second, people may have strategic reasons for accepting this situation, for example PhD students must invest much effort in their jobs in return for low job security and low pay, but such jobs constitute indispensable stepping stones for future appointment as a tenured professor. Taking a PhD is therefore an investment in one's career, as without such a degree it is virtually impossible to work in academia. Third, people may possess a personal pattern of coping with the demands at work that reflect a strong desire to be approved of. Such "overcommitted" people will respond inflexibly to high effort-low reward situations and will therefore be more prone to experiencing strain than less committed persons.

Several review studies have supported the idea that effort-reward imbalance yields adverse outcomes for health and well-being. Workers reporting high imbalance tended to experience more cardiovascular complaints, obtained higher scores on risk factors for such complaints (e.g. elevated cholesterol levels and hypertension) and reported lower well-being (especially burnout) than others. Overcommitment was also related to adverse outcomes; indeed, the risk of getting a cardiovascular disease or even dying from such a disease was 1.2 to as much as 4.5 times higher for highly overcommitted workers. Further, both overcommitment and imbalance were associated with a suboptimally functioning immune system: overcommitted workers and workers experiencing imbalance simply got sick more often than others.[9,10]

Obviously, a good balance between the effort workers invest in their jobs and the rewards received in return for these efforts is important for worker health and well-being. From a practical point of view, this model emphasizes the importance of having an equitable balance between effort (job demands) and rewards (money, approval and job security/career opportunities). Organizations attempting to improve well-being could therefore focus on decreasing the effort employees must invest in their jobs or on improving their rewards: improve pay rates, job security and degree to which they experience approval.

VITAMINS, DEMANDS AND RESOURCES

The models discussed earlier have been (and still are) extremely important in how we think about jobs, their design and their effects on worker health and well-being. Although other models are perhaps not as popular, influential or innovative, some of these deserve to be mentioned here as well. For instance, the earlier discussion may suggest that having much autonomy, variety, contact with others, et cetera in a job is always desirable – the more the better. However, according to Peter Warr from the University of Sheffield, the effects of the characteristics of a job on performance and well-being are similar to those of vitamins on health. At low intake, vitamin deficiencies lead to physiological impairment and ill-health. However, after the recommended daily dose has been reached, there is no benefit from taking additional quantities. Indeed, some vitamins may actually be harmful when taken in very large quantities. For example, take too much vitamin A for a long time, and your liver and bones will suffer, while there are no known adverse effects of taking too much vitamin E. Peter Warr's *Vitamin model* proposes that work characteristics behave like vitamins. The absence of particular work characteristics always leads to certain forms of unhappiness, but the presence of such characteristics beyond a certain level will not further increase happiness (like overdosing vitamin E) or may even be harmful (like taking too much vitamin A).[11] This reasoning is interesting and important, as it shows that a well-designed job needs variety, autonomy and skill discretion, demands, contact with others, et cetera, but only up to a certain level: having too much of an initially good thing will not yield the desired outcomes and may even backfire.

Finally, the approaches discussed earlier all focus on particular sets of job characteristics, for example demands, control, support and variety. However, these characteristics are not necessarily equally important for productivity and well-being across *all* jobs, and neither do the models discussed earlier include *all* characteristics that are important for productivity, motivation and well-being in specific jobs. One might therefore reason that it is best to discard any *a priori* ideas about fixed sets of specific work characteristics that are universally important across all jobs. Rather, the characteristics that are particularly relevant for worker productivity, motivation and well-being may vary across jobs. For example, in a nurse's job, emotional support will be important due to the high level of emotional demands in such a job, but this type of support will be considerably less important in, say, the job of an architect.

These ideas led to the development of the *Job Demands-Resources model* in the early 2000s.[12] This model distinguishes among two broad classes of job characteristics. On the one hand, there are the *demands* of the job. High demands are particularly strongly associated with strain and ill-health, such as burnout. On the other hand, a job will also contain *resources*, defined as the aspects of the job that may help in achieving work goals, reduce job demands and the associated physiological and psychological costs, and/or stimulate personal growth and development. Job characteristics such as the presence of social support, skill discretion, autonomy, feedback, job security and monetary rewards fall within this category. Resources are particularly strongly associated with motivation (work engagement).

Similar to Karasek's Job-Demands-Control model, the adverse effects of high demands are presumed to be weaker or to become positive in the presence of high levels of resources. Since studies using this model often focus on the job characteristics that are included in the models proposed by Hackman and Oldham, Robert Karasek and Johannes Siegrist, it is not surprising that the demands-resources model has received a similar degree of empirical support.[13] Compared with other approaches, the best features of this model are probably its simplicity and flexibility: it can be used across many different types of jobs and can incorporate all sorts of job and even personal characteristics.

WORK CHARACTERISTICS AND HAPPINESS: THE ROLE OF MOTIVATION

The models discussed in this chapter often assume that the presence of high demands and the absence of valued job characteristics such as social support and job control are inherently stressful, because they make it difficult to obtain a job's goals. From a different point of view, researchers have argued that working can satisfy various basic human needs, and that the degree to which these are fulfilled affects employee functioning. The *self-determination theory* developed by Richard Ryan and Edward Deci distinguishes three such needs, namely (1) the *need for autonomy*, representing individuals' desire to experience a sense of choice and volition; (2) the *need for relatedness*, referring to the need for experiencing positive relationships with others and mutual respect, caring and reliance; and (3) the *need for competence*, referring to the need for accomplishing challenging tasks successfully and obtaining desired results.[14]

Research has shown that satisfaction of these needs is associated with positive outcomes, such as task persistence, high performance, satisfaction, organizational commitment and psychological well-being.[15] Most important, satisfaction of these needs leads to high levels of *autonomous motivation*. Workers with a high degree of autonomous motivation engage in work because they want to and choose to do so; they are interested in their jobs, enjoy performing their tasks and consider these personally important. Also note that autonomous motivation is largely the opposite of *extrinsic motivation*, where workers solely engage in a particular behaviour or action in order to receive an external reward (e.g. a salary or a bonus) or to avoid being punished.

All forms of motivation may result in high performance, but only the autonomous type of motivation also results in high levels worker happiness and well-being.[16]

Belgian and Dutch psychologists showed that the presence of job resources (such as social support and autonomy) and the absence of high demands were associated with higher satisfaction of the three basic needs mentioned earlier. Moreover, frustration of these needs related to lower happiness, as evidenced by higher levels of burnout and lower levels of engagement. Moreover, high levels of engagement and low levels of burnout were associated with more autonomous and less extrinsic motivation. Overall, this research shows that the presence of particular job characteristics may satisfy or frustrate the satisfaction of certain basic human needs, in turn affecting the degree to which workers experience happiness – burnout, engagement and autonomous motivation – at work.[17,18]

From a practical point of view, this research suggests that in order to promote productivity and well-being, employers should attempt to maximize their employees' autonomous motivation. Workers who thoroughly like their jobs and who consider their job personally important are more likely to be happy and productive workers. This desirable state may be brought about by increasing the resources and decreasing the demands that are present in a job.

CONCLUSION: PROMOTING HAPPINESS AT WORK

This chapter started from the assumption that employers have good reason to attempt to improve their employees' levels of happiness. The main conclusions of this chapter are first, that jobs can be designed in such a way that both worker happiness and productivity are promoted. By focusing on the right mix of work characteristics, organizations can design jobs that on the one hand motivate workers to work hard and to be productive, and that promote worker well-being and happiness on the other hand. Well-designed jobs will satisfy workers' basic needs, thus increasing their autonomous motivation, productivity and happiness. The effects of work characteristics on worker health should not be underestimated; as we have seen, "unhealthy" jobs may not only affect one's well-being but also substantially increase the chances of dying from cardiovascular disease.

Second, as for which characteristics are most important for promoting happiness and motivation, the approaches discussed in this chapter provide different recommendations. However, two job features stand out as especially important. The first is the degree to which workers can maintain meaningful interactions with others. Consistent with the ideas of the human relations movement, the quality of the social relations at work – with colleagues, supervisors, clients, students, et cetera – is of major importance in determining worker happiness. The second is the degree to which workers can influence their work; central concepts here are autonomy, skill discretion and job control. Importantly, the finding that increasing job control promotes worker happiness and performance speaks against Frederick Taylor's central principle that in order to boost worker performance, the planning of the tasks should be separated from their execution (Chapter 2). The essence of having a high degree of control is that it allows workers to plan their tasks themselves, implying that the "one best way" envisaged by Taylor does not exist. Rather, it appears that workers should be allowed to experiment with different ways of doing their tasks, deciding for themselves what works best for them. This will increase their motivation, skills, happiness and productivity.

Third, just as taking London Underground's Victoria line is not the only way to get from Walthamstow to Pimlico, the overview presented in this chapter shows that there are many different viewpoints on what constitutes a good, healthy and productive job. Since there are so many models to choose from, designing a job is no easy feat. However, note that the insights offered by different models can easily be combined. Further, the approaches discussed here clearly show how the design of jobs can be *worsened*: focus only on providing financial incentives and neglect worker happiness, deny workers any control over their jobs, make sure that their job is deprived of meaning and significance, et cetera. In this sense, the ideas discussed in this chapter will provide practitioners with useful insights as to how jobs can be improved (or worsened).

Finally, an important caveat here is that this chapter mainly focused on the characteristics of jobs. But jobs are done by people, each with their own characteristics, needs, interests and capacities. A mentally challenged worker in a Dutch work centre was involved in packaging packets of dry instant soup: putting 12 packets in a box, all day long, every day of the week; can a job possibly be more boring? However, when asked whether he found his job sufficiently varied, this worker merrily said, "There is plenty of variation in my work. Monday I was packing tomato soup, today vegetable soup, tomorrow I will be packing chicken soup!" Clearly, a worker's evaluation of a job depends not only on the characteristics of that job, but also on those of the job holder. This points to an important question: how can organizations make sure that the right person is selected for the job?

5

THE BEST POSSIBLE MAN

Optimizing worker-environment fit

The first jigsaw puzzle was constructed around 1760 by the London-based cartographer John Spilsbury. He took one of his world maps, pasted it to a sheet of wood and carved out each country to create a "dissected map". By doing so, he created an educational toy that has helped children learn geography ever since. Puzzles for adults emerged only around the 1900s. The hardest puzzle in the world is said to be a 340-piece puzzle featuring Jackson Pollock's action painting *Convergence*, an abstract and impressionistic collage of colours – black, white, red, yellow, traces of blue – splattered on a canvas.

The essence of a jigsaw puzzle is that each piece can be fitted in the puzzle in just a single way, that is, there should be a perfect fit between its shape and picture and those of the adjacent pieces. Is *Convergence* really the world's most difficult puzzle? Compared with other jigsaw puzzles it may well be, especially in its current 1,000-piece re-issue. However, as many managers and human resources professionals will testify, finding the right person for a particular job opening in an organization – the person who fits in well and who makes the organization complete – may be at least as confusing as and will often take much more time than completing a jigsaw puzzle.

This chapter discusses psychological perspectives on finding the right person for a particular position in the organization. Where

Chapters 2 and 3 discussed tasks and remuneration practices as the focal points for optimizing work performance, worker characteristics (their basic needs, happiness and motivations) were considered in Chapters 3 and 4. The current chapter combines these two viewpoints, focusing on the optimization of the fit between the worker and his or her work environment. The basic assumption here is that some workers will be better suited for a particular position than others in terms of their interests, personality, capacities, et cetera. The challenge, then, is to make sure that all positions are occupied by workers who fit that position well, like correctly-placed pieces of a puzzle. This is the area of recruitment, assessment and selection of workers; of the measurement of personality characteristics and skills; and on-the-job training and schooling. Around 1900, these topics were by no means unknown to managers and employers. Frederick Taylor was already familiar with the idea that not all workers were equally well suited for all types of jobs, not even if they possessed the right physical capacities for a particular job. For example, the workers he hired to handle pig iron as a regular occupation were required to be strong, but should also "resemble the ox" in their "mental make-up".[1] However, a systematic, well-integrated and psychological view on these issues was still lacking.

PSYCHOTECHNICS: APPLYING PSYCHOLOGY TO REAL LIFE

Born in 1863 as the third son of a successful lumber merchant in the Prussian port of Dantzig (now Gdansk in Poland), Hugo Münsterberg entered the University of Leipzig in 1883. After attending a lecture by the eminent psychologist Wilhelm Wundt (who had opened the world's first psychological laboratory in 1879), Münsterberg pursued a PhD in physiological psychology in 1885 under Wundt's supervision. After obtaining this degree, he started as a teacher at the University of Freiburg. Here Münsterberg had a psychological laboratory – housed in two rooms of his private apartment – where he conducted research in the area of cognitive psychology, studying topics such as attention, memory and learning.[2] He was promoted to Assistant Professor in 1891. After meeting the famous Harvard psychology professor William James at a scientific congress, James invited him to Harvard to assume leadership of its psychological laboratory. After a brief return to Freiburg in 1895, Münsterberg was re-appointed as a full professor at Harvard in 1897, working in its psychological laboratory and taking on various important positions such as that of President of the American Psychological Association.

At the time, Münsterberg was well-known among both the scientific community and the general public, as he enthusiastically practiced his belief that psychologists should apply the insights obtained in psychological studies to real-life situations. Münsterberg coined the term psychotechnics for such applications, since – like other technical sciences – psychology "teaches us to apply theoretical knowledge for the furtherance of human purposes. (It) tells us what we ought to do if we want to reach certain ends".[3] He wrote extensively about these applications in a wide diversity of areas such as forensics, marketing, spiritualism, politics, film theory and women. Münsterberg must have been literally everywhere, sometimes to the annoyance of others. In 1909, an anonymous writer penned a five-couplet poem about him, containing the quite funny lines

> There is nothing in the universe
> on which he has not gravely touched
> and always he appears to curse
> what we have long and fondly clutched
> . . .
> I live in constant fear that he
> whose wisdom seems to reach so far
> some morning may decide that we
> have no right to be what we are.[2]

MÜNSTERBERG AND INDUSTRIAL PSYCHOLOGY

To our purposes, Munsterberg's contributions to industrial psychology are most important. An ardent admirer of Frederick Taylor, Münsterberg aimed to "sketch the outlines of a new science which is to intermediate between the modern laboratory psychology and the problems of economics: the psychological experiment is systematically to be placed at the service of commerce and industry". One might say that what Taylor had done for the body of the worker, Münsterberg attempted do for the worker's mind. In his work on industrial and vocational psychology, he argued that psychotechnics should address three main issues: "we ask how to find the best possible man, how to produce the best possible work, and how to secure the best possible effects".[3]

Finding the best possible man

In dealing with first issue − how to find the best possible man − Münsterberg proposed four main steps. The first step is to determine which goals should be achieved in a job. He argued that the activities that make up a job are actually ways of satisfying human demands (or needs). These demands could be those of the worker himself: Münsterberg distinguished between *selfish demands* (such as the demands for support, luxury, power, honour, pleasure) and *ideal demands* (truth, beauty, morality, progress, justice and religion). These demands could also be those of their fellow men. Here we have *public demands* (including the needs for government, law, protection, education and hygiene) and *individual demands* (food, clothing, shelter, transportation, health and entertainment). In order to perform well in a job, workers should possess the right *knowledge* as well as have the *ability* to conduct the job. However, they should also have an *interest* in the demands to be fulfilled in order to derive satisfaction from doing that job.

The second step is to determine which knowledge and abilities are needed to perform well in that job. For example, a civil engineer would fulfil the demand of his fellow men for transportation. He should therefore know the science of engineering (knowledge) and also have the ability and training to put this knowledge into practice (skills). However, in order to be successful, an engineer should also have some knowledge of business, finance, architecture and art history, as his creations should not only be built but also be financed and maintained, and should be pleasing to the eye.

The third step is to see whether workers who were interested in taking this job were well suited for the tasks. The psychotechnical method aimed to select "those personalities which by their mental qualities are especially fit for a particular kind of economic work". In this context, "personality" referred to personality traits but also to intelligence, skills, knowledge and experience. Just like today, when hiring new staff, it was common for employers to rely on evidence that applicants possessed the desired knowledge and skills, such as testimonials from former employers, certificates referring to previous education and – of course – personal impressions of the applicant. But Münsterberg felt that whereas such procedures could perhaps secure the elimination of the entirely unfit, they could not uncover "the true qualities of the mind and the deeper traits".

Another way to shed light on these personalities was by the then well-used method of introspection, that is, by asking people to think about themselves and have them answering questions like "Do you smile naturally and easily and feel the smile in your heart, or is your face ordinarily expressionless?" and "Do you show your good-will and affection, or are you keeping them bottled up for use in some future epoch, or on another planet, or after the funerals of your relatives and friends?"[4] Münsterberg acknowledged that such methods could have some use in helping young people choose a vocation that was right for them, but also pointed out that their utility was limited, since only people who already know themselves well would be able answer such questions correctly – in which case these tests were superfluous.

He therefore argued that "the method of ordinary self-observation [should be replaced] by objective experiment in the psychological laboratory", where reaction times, memory capacity, the ability to profit from training and other properties relevant to task execution could objectively and scientifically be recorded. The psychotechnical problem was therefore

> to analyze definite economic tasks with reference to the mental qualities which are necessary or desirable for them, and we have to find methods by which these mental qualities can be tested . . . both sides, the vocational demands and the personal function, are examined with equal scientific thoroughness.

For instance, Münsterberg devised an attention test in which 30 female participants were given a page from that morning's newspaper. At the signal of the experimenter, the women had 6 minutes to cross out every "a" on that page. Individual differences in attention were established by examining how many letters were crossed out and overlooked. Participants could then be compared and ranked on the basis of their test performance.[2] Thus, the third step involved the mapping of a person's suitability for the job – not on the basis of introspection or subjective impressions and not even using Frederick Taylor's "scientific" selection of the workman (Chapter 2), but using the insights obtained in the psychological laboratory using experimental tests that were specifically devised to tap personal characteristics deemed relevant for the job. By comparing applicants' performance on these tests, an employer could find the best possible person for the job.

The best possible work and the best possible effects

As for the two other goals of industrial psychology (how to produce the best possible work and how to secure the best possible effects), Münsterberg gave considerably less attention to these issues. When the best possible man for the job was found, learning and training could make sure that this person's knowledge and mental capacities were tailored to the specific job to be conducted, resulting in the best possible man for the job producing the best possible work. In order to produce the best possible effects, everything which diminished efficiency at work should be removed, whereas everything that could increase efficiency should be introduced. Münsterberg cites Frederick Taylor's scientific management approach and the time-and-motion studies devised by the Gilbreths as prime examples of increasing efficiency, with the latter dealing with the "limitless waste of human motions and psychophysiological efforts". Münsterberg further acknowledged that some jobs could be extremely boring, but this could be addressed by selecting "men and women whose mental dispositions favor an easy grasp of successive uniform impressions" (i.e. who can stand repetitive, boring work) for the job.

Hugo Münsterberg passed away in 1916 at age 53, in the midst of delivering a lecture. However, during his relatively short life span, he profoundly changed the face of psychology. Whereas psychology was formerly a somewhat obscure and self-focused branch of science that confined itself to conducting intricate experiments in the laboratory, Münsterberg had turned it into a discipline that was widely considered to have the potential to make a significant contribution to the betterment of everyday life. This was especially clear in the area of industrial psychology. Here he was among the first to plea for a scientific and experimental study of worker "personalities", to show how jobs could be analyzed systematically in terms of their requirements and to emphasize that there should be a good fit between the job and the worker. Nowhere is his influence more visible than in the field of personnel psychology, focusing on the analysis and design of jobs and the assessment, selection and training of workers. Especially the latter set of topics tends to attract much interest from the lay public, probably because almost everyone is confronted with this aspect of personnel psychology – either as employer, professional or applicant. The remainder of this chapter therefore focuses on current insights in the assessment of personality and skills, and the effectiveness of employee training programmes.

FINDING THE BEST POSSIBLE MAN: KNOWLEDGE, SKILLS, ABILITIES AND OTHER CHARACTERISTICS

In the decades after Münsterberg, psychologists working in the area of selection and assessment have agreed on four broad categories of characteristics (sometimes referred to as *competencies*) that are relevant for employee functioning: knowledge, skills, abilities and "other characteristics" (abbreviated as KSAOs). These four classes of characteristics may be considered a more formalized and extended version of the terms used by Münsterberg.

- *Knowledge* refers to the degree to which a candidate possesses an organized body of information (i.e. is aware of facts and procedures) which, if applied, allows for adequate performance on the job. For example, a door-to-door salesperson selling vacuum cleaners should be familiar with the characteristics of the product she or he sells (How does it work? Does the user risk electrocution when it is used on a wet floor?).
- *Skills* refer to the degree to which candidates can successfully manipulate people, data, things and ideas. For example, our door-to-door salesperson must possess interpersonal skills, such as convincing a prospective customer that *now* is the right time to buy *this* vacuum cleaner.
- *Ability* is the capacity to learn a certain physical, mental or psycho-motor activity (i.e. skill). For instance, mental ability is the ability to learn mental skills: any good salesperson should be able to learn to set goals for himself or herself and to deal effectively with prospective customers. Similarly, only few of us will have the physical ability to learn the skills needed to become a top athlete.
- The class of *other personal characteristics* includes attitudes, beliefs, personality characteristics and values. Door-to-door salespersons will be more successful if they are not overly concerned with moral and ethical principles (they should make that deal, whether or not the customer can afford a new vacuum cleaner), cope well with disappointments (most contacts with prospective customers will not result in a sale) and are persistent (they should not take "no" for an answer).

The key to successful selection is to make sure that a particular job is filled by a candidate who possesses a combination of KSAOs that fits well with the tasks to be conducted. In practice, this often means that applicants are subjected to all sorts of instruments that are designed to show to which degree they have the right characteristics for the job – interviews, psychological and intelligence tests, assessment centres, et cetera.

Personality at work

So far, we have spoken about "personality" without providing an explicit definition of this concept. Simply put, a person's personality refers to the thoughts, feelings and behaviours that are associated with this person. If such behaviours and feelings are stable across time, they are referred to as *personality traits*. Conversely, if these behaviours and feelings are only temporary and depend on a person's situation at a particular time, they are called *states* (e.g. moods). One might say that traits are the rule, while states are exceptions to that rule. In the following, we refer to these stable personality traits when talking about personality.

It is quite common for employees to be subjected to personality tests in some stage of their career – whether this is in the stage of applying for a particular position (recruitment) or even before that (vocational counselling), in the middle of their career (e.g. when thinking about a possible new step within the organization) or when one's contract with a particular organization comes to an end (as part of an outplacement procedure). However, this has not always been the case. An influential review study published by psychologists Robert Guion and Richard Gottier in 1965 recommended that "Personality measures should not be used for selection decisions unless their validity has been specifically and competently determined for the specific situation".[5] The validity of a psychological test refers to the degree to which it measures accurately and reliably what it should measure, and is therefore a key feature of any psychological test. Since that same review had shown that there was little evidence for the validity of personality measures in personnel selection, this recommendation could have been a death warrant for the use of such tests.

However, in the decades that followed, hundreds of research articles were published, attempting to demonstrate the validity of personality tests by showing that such tests could predict job performance, using a wide variety of personality constructs and performance criteria and among many diverse jobs and occupations. The integration of this literature was greatly facilitated by the development of the "five factor model" (FFM) of personality. Around 1990, many researchers in this area had accepted the idea that five major dimensions could adequately represent most, if not all, of the personality constructs that had been studied at the time.[6] These so-called *big five* are (1) *Openness to experience* (incorporating features such as being intellectually curious, sensitive to beauty and willing to try new things); (2) *Conscientiousness* (being efficient, hardworking, dependable and responsible); (3) *Extraversion* (being active, assertive, talkative, warm and gregarious); (4) *Agreeableness* (being kind, altruistic, generous, forgiving, modest and straightforward); and (5) *Neuroticism* (referring to feelings of anxiety, being tense and emotionally unstable and being hostile to others). Note that these five factors will not always be equally important for job performance. While possessing a high degree of openness to experience may be important for artists or university professors, it may be less relevant to the performance of nurses. Extraversion will be a desirable trait for politicians (or door-to-door salespersons) but not so for house cleaners. This implies that – consistent with the ideas of Münsterberg – different jobs require different patterns of personality characteristics: who is the best man for a job depends on the characteristics of both the job and the man.

Focusing on the big five factors, management researchers Murray Barrick and Michael Mount summarized the findings on the associations between personality and work performance obtained in 162 samples.[7] They found that the factors of the FFM accounted from a negligibly small 0.15 per cent (for openness to experience) to a relatively decent 4.8 per cent (for conscientiousness) of the differences in performance of the participants. Although even the latter figure may seem relatively modest, these findings presented a considerably more optimistic view of the value of including personality measures in personnel selection procedures than that of Guion and Gottier, providing considerable utility to personnel selection decisions.[8]

Mental ability tests

"Intelligence" (or "general mental ability") is the general trait that is measured by cognitive ability tests, focusing on for example verbal and mathematical ability, problem solving capacity, reasoning, perception and memory. These abilities can often be further divided in even more specific subtests, for example, there are verbal, non-verbal, logical and numerical reasoning tests. Apparently, there is no single type of intelligence, and which type is most relevant for a particular job may vary. However, this does not mean that no general conclusions on the associations between intelligence and job performance can be drawn.

Lay people are sometimes surprised to learn that intelligence is a major determinant of job performance. Psychologists John Hunter and Frank Schmidt argue that this is because people greatly underestimate the differences in the performance of workers.[9] According to Hunter and Schmidt, for low-complexity jobs (such as routine blue-collar and clerical jobs) the most productive 1 per cent of the workers is not less than 53 per cent more productive than the *average* worker in such jobs. For medium-complexity jobs (e.g. crafts and decision-making clerical jobs) this difference increases to 88 per cent. Thus, within jobs there are vast differences in the productivity of individual workers. Importantly, these differences in productivity can be linked to differences in general mental ability: about 28 per cent of the differences in the performance of people holding the same job is accounted for by differences in general intelligence, presumably because general cognitive ability is a powerful predictor of the ability to acquire new knowledge and skills.[10] Thus, when selecting workers, organizations are well-advised to consider general intelligence as part of the selection process for both manual and mental jobs.

Emotional intelligence

At present, the debate as to whether general intelligence matters for job performance is largely over. Instead, since the 2000s a different type of intelligence has attracted considerable attention from researchers as well as the lay public. *Emotional intelligence* (EI) can be defined as "the set of abilities (verbal and nonverbal) that enable a person to generate, recognize, express, understand, and evaluate their own, and others, emotions in order to guide thinking and action successfully cope with environmental demands".[11] Since many workers must deal with people – supervisors, subordinates, clients, patients, customers – EI could well influence job performance.

Current research tends to agree with this idea. For example, in a study of 257 South Korean retail store managers and their 1,611 subordinates, a Dutch-Korean team of researchers found that the manager's EI was related to store cohesiveness, relating to the degree to which employees show that they care for each other and that they feel a sense of belonging to the store. In turn, store cohesiveness was related to the sales-directed behaviour of frontline employees, which ultimately predicted the financial performance of the stores.[12] A meta-analysis of 43 studies that incorporated data from almost 6,000 workers showed that EI accounted for 6 to 9 per cent of the differences in worker performance, as rated by their supervisors.[13] Consequently, it seems fair to conclude that EI is an important predictor of job performance as well.

Employment interviews

Nearly all organizations use employment interviews for selection purposes. Such interviews are intended to predict future job performance on the basis of a participant's answers to the questions posed by the members of a selection committee. Supervisors and human resource practitioners prefer this approach to other selection procedures, and applicants perceive interviews as fair as compared with other methods.[14] That is excellent news, but how useful are interviews as a selection tool? Can the subjective impressions formed by an interviewer that are in turn based on the possibly self-promotional responses of a job applicant really provide a realistic estimate of the latter's suitability for a position? Is this a reliable and valid way to find Münsterberg's best possible man for the job?

In an early review study that was published in 1949, Ralph Wagner from the then just-founded American Institutes for Research summarized the findings of 106 articles on the validity and reliability of employment interviews. His main conclusions were that (1) the validity and reliability of the interview were highly specific to both the situation and the interviewer, that is, in *some* situations and for *some* interviewers the interview worked well, but not in other situations or for other interviewers; (2) interviews should be used only for evaluating factors that could not be measured accurately by other methods; (3) interviews are most accurate when a standardized set of questions is used; (4) interviewers should be skilled in eliciting complete information from the applicant and in observing his or her behaviour, suggesting that job interviews should not be conducted by well-meaning amateurs but rather by professionals; and (5) more quantitative research on the interview was much needed.[15]

Wagner's call for more research did not go unheeded: over the last decades, the number of papers published on the job interview increased with time and several review studies have summarized their findings. One landmark review study was based on data from 25,244 individuals, finding that the scores of participants on a job interview accounted for on average 13 per cent of their differences in job performance. Structured interviews (with interviewers taking notes, using standardized scoring guides to assess candidates) predicted performance better than unstructured interviews (accounting for 16 versus 9 per cent of the differences in performance, respectively). Interestingly, the content of the interviews mattered. Interviews focusing on obtaining information about how a person would behave in a hypothetical situation (e.g. whether she or he would rather win a coveted award for lowering costs than help a co-worker who will make a significant profit for the company) accounted for a larger part of the differences in performance than interviews focusing on actual past behaviours on the job, and interviews intended to assess psychological traits such as dependability (25 per cent, 16 per cent and 9 per cent, respectively).[16] Later studies have confirmed these notions, showing that employment interviews can be useful in the selection process, especially if these interviews are well-structured and focus on obtaining situational information rather than job-related or psychological information.

Assessment centres

An assessment centre is simply a collection of various instruments that can be used to assess a person's KSAOs in relation to a particular job. Usually it consists of a combination of personality and cognitive ability tests, an interview and one or more practical exercises. A candidate's performance is discussed by one or more assessors who rate that performance. In turn, these ratings are used for hire/promotion decisions or to give developmental feedback to the candidate. The distinguishing feature of the assessment centre vis-à-vis other assessment approaches is the inclusion of practical exercises. One such exercise is the *role playing exercise* in which the candidate takes on the role of a manager who must deal with a subordinate who must be motivated for a task (tapping one's motivational and leadership skills) or that of a salesperson who must sell a product to a customer (focusing on one's commercial and interpersonal skills). The *in-basket exercise* simulates the paperwork that arrives in the mailbox or on the desk of a manager. Candidates receive a packet of information that they must read, prioritize and address to resolve issues. This exercise aims to measure a candidate's time-management, planning and other management skills. There is the *leaderless group discussion exercise*, in which participants must – within a set period of time – work in an unstructured group to resolve given problems, assessing interpersonal and cooperative skills. A final type of exercise involves the analysis of an organizational problem; the applicant is then to prepare a written set of recommendations (this is a *case analysis exercise*) or give an oral presentation (a *presentation exercise*) about it for higher management. In these exercises, managerial skills in the area of problem solving, strategic planning and information processing are tested.

Of course, the content of an assessment centre will usually be matched closely with the job for which a candidate is hired. By combining such exercises with more traditional measures to map a participant's characteristics, the assessment centre intends to increase the predictive value of the selection procedure. A review of 69 studies that examined the predictive value of the five types of assessment exercises discussed earlier showed that differences in the scores on each of these exercises accounted for on average 2 to 4 per cent of the differences in individual job performance, with the case analysis and oral presentation exercises showing the strongest relations with job performance.[17] However, the proof of the pudding is whether such exercises really add to the prediction of job performance, beyond what is already accounted for by more traditional approaches such as cognitive ability and personality tests.

Comparison of approaches to find the best possible man

This chapter presented a discussion of various approaches to measure the degree to which workers possess the KSAOs needed to perform well in a particular job. As this overview showed, participants' scores on cognitive ability tests are usually a strong predictor of their job performance, accounting for on average 28 per cent of the differences in their performance. Employment interviews come in second, accounting for 9 per cent (for unstructured interviews) to 16 per cent (for structured interviews) of the differences in performance. Emotional intelligence accounts for 6 to 9 per cent of these performance differences. The big five personality dimensions account for a meagre 0.15 per cent (for openness to experience) to a modest 4.8 per cent (conscientiousness) of differences in performance. Finally, exercises that are commonly included in assessment centres account for 2 to 4 per cent of the variations in job performance.

Importantly, these figures cannot simply be added to arrive at an overall estimate of how much of the differences in job performance can be accounted for by using these selection approaches, as these tend to overlap to some degree. For example, emotional intelligence will to some degree tap the same concept as, say, agreeableness or the leaderless group discussion exercise. The effects of these concepts on performance are therefore not independent. Since cognitive ability is the strongest predictor of performance, it makes sense to start from here in examining whether the other assessment methods are useful: do personality, assessment exercises, emotional intelligence and employment interviews contribute to the explanation of individual differences in performance, *beyond* what is already accounted for by intelligence?

This question was addressed by Frank Schmidt and John Hunter. They showed that general mental ability accounted for 25 per cent of the differences in job performance. If both general mental ability and conscientiousness were considered, 36 per cent of the differences in performance could be accounted for, that is, conscientiousness accounted for an additional 11 per cent of the differences in performance. Structured employment interviews accounted for 15 per cent of the variance in performance, beyond cognitive ability. Inclusion of practical exercises (as in an assessment centre) accounted for a relatively small 3 per cent of the differences in performance, beyond cognitive ability.[18] This relatively low incremental value of assessment centre exercises was confirmed in a later study, finding that the inclusion of assessment exercises accounted for an additional 3 per cent of the differences in performance, beyond mental ability and the big five factors. Of the five types of exercises considered in that study, only case analysis and role playing exercises were related to performance, taking differences in personality and intelligence into account.[17] None of these studies included emotional intelligence. However, a recent review study found that cognitive ability and the big five personality factors accounted for on average 42 per cent of the differences in performance, and that addition of a measure of emotional intelligence improved this figure with 5 to 7 per cent, which seems certainly worthwhile.[13]

Overall, one may conclude from this overview that the best possible man for a job can best be found by using a combination of a general mental ability test, a test of conscientiousness, a structured job interview and – if needed for the job – an emotional intelligence test. Assessment centre exercises may be included as well, but this may not be cost-efficient when considering their contribution to the prediction of job performance and their inclusion will therefore often be contingent upon other considerations than cost-effectiveness. For example, candidates for higher-level jobs often consider assessment centre exercises as more acceptable than mental ability tests.

RIGHT PERSON, RIGHT POSITION: IMPROVING PERSON-ENVIRONMENT FIT

Taking the ideas of Hugo Münsterberg as a starting point, this chapter discussed the idea that in order to achieve high job performance, there should be a match between the characteristics of a job and those of a worker. Using job analysis, the features needed to perform well in that job can be identified. Employers can successively determine the suitability of candidates for that position using instruments such as intelligence and personality tests, assessment centres and employment interviews. In this way, the best man for the job can be selected, potentially leading to the best possible work and best possible effects.

Training and schooling

Note that even the *best possible* person for the job may not be *well suited* for the job. That is, employees may well have the physical and/or mental abilities to do the job, but may not (yet) possess the knowledge and skills needed to perform well. This is usually no problem if employers are willing to invest in further schooling and training of workers. Indeed, this is often a necessity since nowadays work routines and equipment change faster than ever. However, workers do not always perform differently on the job after attending a training: learning in a training experience is rarely sufficient to render that training effective. Rather, the paramount concern of organizational training efforts is whether the learning that results from a training experience "transfers" to the job and leads to meaningful chances in work performance. In practice, this is not always the case, and research has focused on the factors that hinder or promote such transfer.

A review of 89 studies found that especially participants obtaining high scores on cognitive ability and conscientiousness, and participants having a supportive work environment, showed a high level of transfer, with each of these factors accounting for 10 to 15 per cent of individual differences in transfer.[19] Moreover, the effects of these factors on the degree of transfer were weaker for so-called closed skills, that is, programmes in which trainees must adopt the modelled behaviours in the same form as they are presented in training and participants have little choice as to what and how to apply the trained principles to the job. For example, there is little leeway permitted in safely operating a power tool. However, with open skills – such as interpersonal or leadership training – the goal is more to inculcate generalizable rules, concepts and principles, and trainees must formulate their own plan on how to apply these rules when at work. They therefore have more choice as to what and how to apply these rules, principles and concepts to the job, meaning that the effects of variables such as general mental ability and conscientiousness on training transfer may become more substantial.

CONCLUSION

This chapter started off by comparing the organization to a jigsaw puzzle with its employees as its pieces. At this point, it has become clear that this comparison is warranted to an only limited degree. Whereas in traditional puzzles, each piece will fit the puzzle in just one correct way and there is only one single way to complete the puzzle, organizations must first decide what sort of piece is needed (through a job analysis), after which the best-fitting piece must be found (through selection and assessment). The best-fitting piece may still not fit the puzzle well, in which organizations may either decide to cut this piece to size using schooling and training, or that the puzzle should be completed in a different way (e.g. when a newly-hired CEO's vision for the organization diverges from that of the former leader of the organization). And whereas not completing a jigsaw puzzle correctly is no major issue, hiring the wrong person for the job may have dire consequences for the organization. Evidently, Pollock's *Convergence* is not the world's most difficult puzzle!

Hugo Münsterberg aimed to find the best possible person to produce the best possible work with the best possible effects. Application of his ideas (and those of other management consultants like Frederick Taylor, Frank and Lillian Gilbreth, et cetera) may well lead to a high-performing and efficient organization. But how about the workers in these organizations? Working hard is fine, but how can we avoid the possible adverse effects of working *too* hard?

6

THE SEVENTH DAY

Recovery from work

According to the Old Testament, God created heaven and earth in six busy days. However, on the seventh day He rested from his work, and the Fourth commandment instructs people to do the same; believers nor their family, servants, cattle or even "strangers within their gates" should work on that day. The Quran does not mention any specific day for resting from work. Although Allah also used six days to create the world, on the seventh He "established himself above the Throne" – business as usual here. Blissfully, He made the night a covering for His followers to sleep and rest in.

Nonbelievers need not worry. In the absence of sacred texts telling them when to rest from work and that work and rest should be alternated, a large body of scientific research has considered the balance between work, work effort and working hours on the one hand, and rest breaks (varying from very short micro-breaks during work to multi-week holidays) on the other. The effects of (disruptions of) this balance have been examined in terms of a wide variety of outcomes such as stress, fatigue, motivation, work performance, sickness absence and burnout, and errors and accidents at work, showing that sufficient recovery from work effort is needed to obtain favourable work outcomes such as high performance and high well-being.

This may seem a trivial insight, and in some ways, it is. For example, the importance of starting a task well-rested was already acknowledged by general Julius Caesar at the battle of Pharsalus in 48 BC. In what was to become the decisive battle in the Roman civil war, Caesar's troops were greatly outnumbered by those of his opponent Pompey the Great. There was much space left between the lines of the two hostile armies. Cleverly, Pompey had ordered his troops to await the attack, trusting that Caesar's soldiers, after running over double the usual ground, would become "weary and exhausted" by the fatigue and would be easier to defeat. However, when Caesar's men noted that their adversaries did not run to meet their charge, they "repressed their speed and halted almost midway so that they would not come up with the enemy when their strength was exhausted".[1] After a short respite they renewed their course. Due to their greater experience and Caesar's superior strategic skills, a huge victory followed, essentially ending the civil war. Briefly afterwards, the Roman senate appointed Caesar *dictator* for ten years. The rest is history.

Clearly, the idea that a world can be won by taking your rest breaks at the right time was not unknown to Caesar and his fellow men. However, the idea that people – soldiers as well as factory workers – must rest at certain intervals to perform optimally had largely disappeared when the industrial revolution took off. Indeed, one of Frederick Taylor's contributions to the organization of modern working life was his observation that workers produced more when they took short breaks from work at certain intervals.[2] This idea was taken further by Lillian and Frank Gilbreth, who devised complicated work/rest schedules, assuming that short and frequent breaks were more beneficial than longer, infrequent breaks.[3] Basically, their assumption was that work performance will improve if workers have opportunities to recover from the effort they expend in completing their tasks. That sounds reasonable, but is it true?

LONG WORKING HOURS, WELL-BEING AND WORK PERFORMANCE

A central concept in the literature on work hours and its consequences is that of *long working hours*. In many Western countries, a regular work week refers to working for on average 32 to 40 hours. For example, in 2015, workers in the European Union worked for on average 36.1 hours per week, with a corresponding figure of 38.6 hours per week for Americans.[4] "Working long hours" refers to a situation in which people work more hours than is widely accepted as being within reasonable bounds, for example the research office of the European Union considers people who on average work longer than 48 hours per week as working long hours. Note that these figures do not include entrepreneurs and small business owners, as these groups decide for themselves how many hours they work, contingent upon their situation and ambition. This does not mean that members of this group always work long hours. For example, the owner of my local guitar store is a former top-level executive of a major international IT corporation who – after accepting a liberal buyout offer – decided to spend more time with his wife, family and hobbies (building and playing guitars, obviously). He now works 4 days a week, some 30 hours in total, and would not dream of going back to his old working schedule as a successful top manager.

Working long hours has a bad reputation in terms of its possible consequences for health, performance and well-being. The evidence as to whether that reputation is deserved is somewhat mixed. For example, a Chinese study found that participants who worked more than 60 hours per week were 1.75 to as much as 5.2 times as likely to report burnout symptoms than participants who worked 40 hours per week or fewer.[5] A review paper of 25 large-scale studies involving data from more than 600,000 participants showed that the risk for individuals who work long hours (55 hours per week or more) for coronary heart disease was 13 per cent higher than that for those working standard working hours; the risk for obtaining a stroke was 33 per cent higher.[6] Another review study defined "long working hours" as working on average more than 8 hours per work day, finding that long working hours were associated with a higher risk of depression, anxiety, sleep problems and cardiovascular disease.[7] A study from down under reported that 13.4 per cent of Australian nurses and midwives engaged in harmful daily drinking, and that the risk of doing so was elevated by 17 per cent for those who worked 50 hours or more per week.[8] Simon Folkard and David Lombardi combined the findings of several studies on the relationship between accidents at work (including injuries and fatal accidents), showing that after having been 10 hours on the job or more, the risk for workers to be involved in such accidents doubled (for 10 hours) or even tripled (for 12 hours and more) after having been relatively low for the first 8 hours of their work shift.[9] Finally, writing in 2015, economist John Pencavel from Stanford University reported that the relationship between working hours and output was non-linear. Using data from British munition workers (mostly women, so-called "munitionettes") who were remunerated on the basis of a piece-rate system during World War I, Pencavel found that below a threshold of 49 hours per week, overall productivity was proportional to the number of hours worked on a day. However, above that threshold, the output per hour fell as the number of hours worked increased. Working longer hours still led to an increase of production numbers (more bullets, bombs and grenades to kill the enemy with), but with decreasing efficiency (workers needed increasingly more time to produce each piece of ammunition). Indeed, the total output after 70 hours of work differed little from the output at 56 hours of work. Apparently there is no point in staying longer on the job. Of course, these estimates are limited in their scope (the jobs in a World War I munition plant are very different from most of today's jobs), but they do show a clear correlation between output and working hours.[10]

All this sounds pretty decisive: working longer hours is associated with lower levels of well-being and health (burnout, depression, anxiety, sleep problems, cardiovascular disease), suboptimal behavioural patterns (e.g. drinking), higher injury and accident rates at work and a decreasing efficiency of production. It might therefore be concluded that working long hours has mainly negative consequences for workers and the organizations they work for. However, that conclusion has been challenged for three reasons. First, studies on the associations between working long hours and outcomes could not always unambiguously distinguish between "cause" and "effect". That is, working long hours may well lead to ill-health, but it would also seem likely for physically and/or mentally less healthy workers to restrict their number of working hours. In both cases, a positive association between the number of working hours and worker health will be observed, but it is difficult to say which interpretation it supports. Second, the associations between the number of hours worked and the presumed outcomes thereof may be statistically significant but can still be practically irrelevant. For instance, the chances of being involved in an accident at work may be three times higher for those working 12 hours as compared with those working 8 hours per day, but since the chances to be involved in such accidents are low in the first place, few will (should?) care about tripling these chances. Finally, the associations between long working hours and outcomes tend to differ for male versus female workers, older versus younger workers, workers having well-designed and pleasurable jobs versus other workers, et cetera. For some groups, the adverse effects of working long hours may be considerable, but this may be different for other groups. Apparently, the adverse effects of long working hours are "nuanced", and more research is needed to obtain a fuller understanding of these effects.[11]

All the same, in many countries, policy makers have decided to err on the safe side, implementing legislation intended to put a maximum to employees' working hours (again, the working hours of self-employed and entrepreneurs are usually not covered by such legislation). Effects may be weak, but each work-related injury, accident or spell of sickness absence that is prevented is one more happy worker, one less claim for medical insurance, et cetera – you will get the point.

WORKING HOURS AND HEALTH: EFFORT-RECOVERY THEORY

Even if the deleterious effects of working long hours to health and well-being would be nuanced, it is important to know about the processes that might account for these effects, as this may provide practical handles for addressing possible problems. In psychology, many studies on the effects of long working hours and its outcomes focus on the balance between work effort in general (i.e. not necessarily long working hours) and recovery from that effort. In an influential paper, Dutch psychologists Theo Meijman and Gijsbertus Mulder argued that working unavoidably coincides with effort expenditure: to achieve something at work, you must put your time, motivation and skills in it.[12] This results in an activation of the sympathetic nervous system; this system kicks into action during emergencies (or what the worker subconsciously *perceives* as an emergency, such as a dissatisfied customer, an evaluation talk with the boss, an assignment that is past its deadline, et cetera) and mobilizes the organism to respond to this stressor. By releasing the hormones adrenaline and noradrenaline, it contributes to increased heart rate, blood pressure, muscle strength, mental activity and total energy consumption (which ultimately results in fatigue). When the emergency is past, direct response to the stressor is no longer needed and the parasympathetic nervous system takes over: the organism returns to a quiet and relaxed state that helps in restoring the undesirable and destructive effects of the activation of the sympathetic nervous system. Blood pressure drops, heart rate slows down and energy is restored rather than consumed. The essence of recovery is that the psychophysiological systems that were activated during work return and stabilize to a baseline level in which no special demands are made on the individual.[13]

Lots of jargon here (apologies for that). Fortunately the basic idea is simple: working induces all sorts of physiological and mental reactions, and these must be compensated for by sufficient opportunities for recovery. Now imagine what happens when workers work long hours. On the one hand, this results in a longer exposure to work stressors (More assignments to be completed! More angry customers to be handled! More deadlines to be met!). Indeed, in itself, working long hours will often already be a response to a stressful situation at work, especially a shortage of competent staff. On the other hand, working long hours implies that there is less opportunity for recovery: work more hours, and there will be less time left for leisure and relaxation.

Importantly, the negative effects of lack of recovery after an exhausting day at work may carry over to the following work day. A worker who has not fully recovered from the previous day must expend "compensatory effort" (i.e. work extra hard) to perform adequately the next day. For example, in the 2017 edition of the *Tour de France* (the prestigious annual multi-stage cycling race), the cyclists finishing first and second in the difficult and exhausting eighth stage (the Frenchman Lilian Calmejane and Robert Gesink from the Netherlands, respectively) did not do as well the next day. In the ninth stage, Calmejane finished only 121st (out of 181 participants), while Gesink had a silly accident within 10 kilometres after the start of the stage and had to abandon the race (fatigued people tend to have more accidents than others). As the *Tour* is extremely challenging, both cyclists may have been unable to mobilize the effort needed to continue to perform well after their exceptional achievement of the previous day. After having completed eight demanding stages of the race, their energy resources were simply fully depleted and just one night of recovery was insufficient to resolve this issue.

In the work context, no real issues will occur if people engage in working long hours only now and then, but habitually working such hours will ultimately result in poor health due to lack of recovery (e.g. burnout, cardiovascular complaints). Evidence for this reasoning was already presented in the previous section, showing that long working hours are associated with adverse outcomes. Essentially, effort-recovery theory holds that there is nothing wrong with working hard, as long as there is sufficient opportunity to recover. These recovery opportunities may take on various forms. For example, workers may recover during the work day by taking breaks or by alternating demanding with less demanding tasks. Evidently, this will be more convenient when their job provides them with high levels of job control and variety (see Chapter 4). Recovery may also occur after work, during weekends and during longer periods of respite such as vacations. What do we know about these recovery opportunities and their effectiveness?

RECOVERING FROM WORK, DURING WORK

As said in the introduction to this chapter, early experts on the organization of working life such as Frederick Taylor and the Gilbreths were already familiar with the idea that optimal work performance required that workers must be allowed to take frequent breaks to perform optimally. Actually, Taylor and the Gilbreths did not so much as to *allow* but rather *forced* workers to take breaks, for example, by shutting down assembly lines at given intervals or by leaving blank sections on the conveyor belt, where no product to be handled by the workers was placed.

More modern approaches give workers at least some say in when breaks are taken and (within certain limits) how long these breaks are. For instance, take regular coffee and lunch breaks. In many occupations, workers (especially in professional jobs) have some influence as to the scheduling of such breaks. Some workers may prefer to have lunch behind their computer screen, others go for a walk, yet others have complete freedom in taking breaks as they work from home. Philip Tucker from Swansea University, Wales, conducted a literature review that demonstrated that rest breaks are indeed effective in managing fatigue and maintaining performance. He studied breaks ranging from 5 minutes to a full hour. Rest breaks were most effective if workers used that time to take a short nap (less than 15 minutes) and drank caffeinated coffee afterwards (two regular cups of coffee suffice). Perhaps not surprisingly, short naps were especially effective during night work. The length of the break seems to be irrelevant, perhaps because the optimal length of a break also depends on the task under consideration. Finally, Tucker recommends that workers should be allowed to take rest at the point where they experience heightened fatigue – something that only they themselves can decide upon. In this sense, self-scheduled breaks are more effective than organization-scheduled breaks.[14] In a study among hospitalized workers with severe work-related hand injury in the People's Republic of China, David Lombardi and his colleagues found that the workers who did not take any breaks had been injured after having been on the job for on average two hours. However, the time-to-injury was on average six hours for the workers who had taken breaks – a major difference that shows that not taking breaks may increase the risk of being involved in a work-related accident. As in Tucker's study, the length of the break was irrelevant.[15]

If the length of a rest break is irrelevant for its effects on recovery, why not schedule many very short breaks during the work day rather than just a smaller number of longer breaks? Indeed, such short breaks (of, say, a few minutes at most) may occur spontaneously, for example when workers must switch from one task to another. Workers may also consciously engage in brief non-work activities, for example when daydreaming, drinking a cup of coffee, having a non-work-related chat with a colleague or by checking one's Facebook page. Although such activities are usually not endorsed by organizations, they may help in recovering from work effort. Research on such micro-breaks has shown that these can indeed be effective in reducing work stress and fatigue.[16] However, there is some evidence showing that performance *decreases* immediately after such very short breaks, suggesting that they do not lead to complete recovery.[17]

In conclusion, this research shows that taking breaks during the work day may help in recovering from work effort, leading to lower accident rates, lower stress levels, better mood and better performance. Taking a nap during these breaks may further improve recovery, as might drinking a caffeinated beverage. These beneficial effects especially apply to self-scheduled and to longer breaks: very short breaks do not lead to better performance – but they may improve your mood, which is also something to consider.

RECOVERY FROM WORK OUTSIDE WORKING HOURS

Audrey Hepburn, the movie star of the 1950s and 1960s and later goodwill ambassador for UNICEF, allegedly liked to be alone in her apartment during the weekends: she said that doing so allowed her "to refuel". Although many of us will use our weekends for different activities, these will usually serve the same purpose, namely to refuel or – in our terminology – to *recover* from work. In doing so, the weekend performs the same function as the evening, the night and vacations.

Recovery during the evening and during weekends

According to Sabine Sonnentag, a German expert in the area of recovery from work, it is important for workers to start their jobs well rested and fully recovered. In her research, workers who felt recovered and energetic in the morning were happier (more engaged) and performed better than other workers.[18] This underlines the need to understand which off-job activities contribute to better recovery. Of course, having a good night's rest is important. However, other activities during off-job time may also contribute (or hinder) recovery from work. For instance, some of us may use part of their off-job time to *prepare or finish work at home*. Essentially, this is just a way of working overtime, and it will be clear that there is no restorative value in activities like handling work-related emails, reading or writing reports or making calls with customers from home. The same psycho-physiological systems that were activated at work remain active while at home, meaning that workers simply work longer hours – only at a different location.

Indeed, one might even argue that working from home (outside but also during regular working hours) increases the likelihood for workers to experience conflict between the home and work contexts. "Work-home conflict" occurs when the demands in one context are incompatible with those of the other context, making participation in both roles more difficult. Time spent on the job cannot be spent with your partner or children, and vice versa (this is called time-based conflict). After having had a difficult meeting at work, you may still feel stressed at home (strain-based conflict). At work you may boss people around, but at home your partner and children will not accept that sort of behaviour (role-based conflict).[19] Conflicts between the work and home context will affect your functioning and well-being negatively, and it is likely that such conflicts will occur more often when "work" and "home" are not separated spatially – as when you work from home, in the evenings or during weekends, when your family is around as well. Thus, working from home in the evening or during weekends is a bad idea when it comes to recovering from work.

Apart from sleep and work, workers may also engage in other activities during off-job time. In a series of diary studies (where workers complete detailed diaries during a number of days, documenting their activities, feelings, performance, et cetera), Sonnentag found that engaging in *household and other domestic activities* (such as child care) was largely unrelated to recovery, perhaps because these broad categories comprise activities that are energy depleting (doing the laundry) as well as activities with a high potential for recovery (reading your child a bedtime story or walking the dog). *Passive leisure activities* (such as watching TV or reading a novel) appear to have a modest potential for recovery. Finally, most studies in this area have found that engaging in *active leisure and social activities* (such as physical exercise and sports, attending cultural events, meeting with friends) during evenings and weekends is associated with a high potential for recovery, as evidenced by higher levels of well-being and lower levels of fatigue in the morning.[18]

Recovery during vacation

As a relatively long and uninterrupted period away from work, vacations may hold a large potential for recovery from work. To test this idea, Jessica de Bloom and her colleagues from Nijmegen University conducted a diary study on the effects of having a one-week winter sports vacation on recovery.[20] Participants were recruited through contacting travel agencies and visiting a winter sports fair. They were contacted five times during a 7-week period; two times before, during, and 1, 2 and 4 weeks after their vacation, respectively. No less than 60 per cent of the participants reported a substantial increase in health and well-being during and after their vacation. Unexpectedly, a small group experienced no effect (23 per cent) or even a negative effect of vacation (17 per cent). This was especially so for participants who derived relatively little pleasure from their winter sports activities or who had experienced a negative event during their holiday – for example, getting injured. This study is interesting, as it shows that whereas taking a vacation can indeed be an effective means of recovery, it is also important how people *perceive* their vacation: was it a pleasurable experience or not? Quite understandably, recovery will be stronger in the first case. Finally, the beneficial effects of having a vacation should not be overestimated. In the study by De Bloom and colleagues, levels of health and well-being had generally returned to pre-vacation levels during the first week of work resumption. These findings agree with those of other research on the potential of holidays for recovery from work.[18]

In conclusion, research on the effects of recovery from work outside working hours has shown that evenings, weekends and vacations all have potential for recovery from work. The nature of the activities in which people engage is important: working from home during off-job time does not help in recovering from work, whereas engaging in active (and to some degree passive) leisure activities has much more beneficial effects on worker's health and well-being. Taking a vacation is a good idea as well; beneficial effects can already be expected for a brief one-week holiday, although these effects do not seem to last very long.

WORK, WORKING HOURS AND RECOVERY

Although the literature on working times, recovery, health and well-being is large and complex, the general insights obtained from this literature mesh well with the recommendations given in the Bible, in the Quran and by Julius Caesar. Use that seventh day for rest and, if that appeals to you, for going to church: engaging in social activities is good for recovery. Alternatively, play a game of rugby with your friends or take a long walk with the dog. The evening and night are excellent opportunities to rest indeed. Taking a break every now and then during your work helps in restoring your energy levels.

Scientific research has supported and refined these ideas. We now know that working long hours – beyond 8 hours a day or so – tends to result in higher accident rates, lower well-being and stagnating productivity. Workers can recover both during and after work. During work, taking very short breaks will largely be ineffective but longer breaks will help maintaining well-being and productivity. After work, engaging in active leisure activities will help you recovering from work, whereas working overtime will not. Taking a long vacation is fine, but in terms of its effects on recovery, a one-week holiday will probably be equally effective. And do not expect miracles – the effects of a vacation wear off fairly soon. The take-home message here is that organizations should offer their employees opportunities to maintain a healthy balance between effort and recovery; in turn, employees are well-advised to use these opportunities to the fullest.

7

THE SHAPE OF THINGS TO COME

Psychology and working life

The widespread introduction of the art of printing books left many a medieval scribe out of work: bibles and other texts were now printed rather than copied. Generally speaking, over the centuries, technological, economic and societal changes have led to the disappearance of many occupations and to major changes in the nature of others. We no longer need switchboard operators to connect us. Lamplighters have become rare. And hear ye: when was the last time you heard a town crier or bellman make his announcements?

THE TIMES, THEY ARE A-CHANGIN'

My grandfather was a postman in the 1960s and 1970s; a decent and secure job that did not pay very well, but well enough to allow him and my grandmother to buy a small house, successfully raising a family of ten. Owing to email, this would be impossible today: where I live, a mail carrier's occupation now is a low-prestige and part-time job that is primarily considered by people wanting to earn a little extra. In the near future, the ongoing introduction of information technology and robots will presumably lead to further computerization (and subsequent disappearance) of many occupations. Writing in 2013, Carl Frey and Michael Osborne from Oxford University ranked

702 occupations on the basis of their likelihood to be computerized.[1] The jobs of surgeons, human resource managers and psychologists were estimated to have a low likelihood to be computerized (less than 1 per cent). However, secretaries and administrative assistants, loan officers and data entry keyers must fear for their jobs, having a 95 per cent or better chance to be computerized in the near future. Today, the best man or woman for the job is to an increasing degree a computer or a robot, especially if there is just one best way of doing that job. Of course, prediction is difficult ("especially about the future", as physicist Niels Bohr added), but it is virtually certain that given enough time, all of us will be confronted with major changes in our jobs due to computerization and robotization.

This is not necessarily a bad thing. If computers and robots take over part of our tasks, they allow us to make better use of our time. Yesterday's bellmen, switchboard operators and lamplighters have found productive employment in other branches of the labour market. The same will happen to today's secretaries, administrative assistants and data entry keyers. However, there is no doubt that a successful transition from such dead-end jobs to jobs offering better perspectives will require considerable flexibility and effort from workers. They are well advised to invest on a life-long basis in their KSAOs in order to remain employable, not only within their current job or within their own organization, but also in the external labour market (other jobs in other organizations). No job is safe from reorganization or bankruptcy: the "long tenure career bargain" is dead.[2] That means taking courses, evening and weekend classes, trying out new procedures at work, et cetera – so much for recovery from work during evenings and weekends! The upside of this development is that, if organizations depend on the knowledge and skills of the workforce, then power rests with those who have the skills, knowledge and insights needed by these companies. Moreover, since organizations strongly depend on their employees' knowledge and skills, they, too, are well advised to invest in the continuous development of their personnel, making sure that workers possess the right skills and knowledge for their jobs.

Against this background of a continuously changing labour market, this book set out to answer two main questions: *why do we work the way we work?* and *how can work performance and worker well-being be optimized — and at what costs?*

OUR WORK, OUR CHOICE: THE RATIONALIZATION OF WORKING LIFE REVISITED

As indicated in Chapter 1, this book is based on four assumptions. The first was that the way we work today is to a large degree due to our views on the best way to put labour to good use, and that we, as society, have a choice as to how we work. Looking at how many of us work and live today, it appears that society has already made that choice a long time ago. More than anything else, we value high productivity and efficiency, leading to more cheap stuff for us to buy and spoil ourselves with. However, this comes at a price as to how labour is organized, directly affecting the quality of our working lives.

As Chapter 2 argued, the basic principles of rationalizing working life, as outlined by Frederick Taylor, Frank and Lillian Gilbreth and their likes, still apply today. That is not because they or the organizations they worked for forced us to accept these principles, but rather because these principles were incredibly attractive to all of us, promising to result in major production increases and, thus, higher incomes for workers and higher profits for factory owners: a classic win-win situation. Taylor and his colleagues delivered: in the past two decades, per-person incomes have increased very substantially (much more stuff for everyone).[3] In this sense, the rationalization of working life has certainly paid off.

Today, Taylor's ideas regarding the best organization of working life are still recognizable in many occupations. Indeed, although initially devised for simple manual jobs, these principles are to an increasing degree used to transform other occupations as well. For example, take a teacher's job. Michael Apple, a professor of education at the University of Wisconsin, argued that teaching is a specific kind of labour process that is currently being subjected to three processes.[4] The first is *rationalization*, that is, teaching policies are to an increasing degree driven by economic considerations such as efficiency and effectiveness, resulting in a weakening of the link between *designing* teaching tasks and actually *conducting* these tasks. Clearly, here we have Taylor's separation between the planning of tasks and their execution. This planning of a teacher's task may well result in a particular, fixed curriculum that teachers should teach: that curriculum is the analogue of Taylor's *one best way* to be followed by that teacher. As Apple and his colleague Susan Jungck reported, "teachers often employed a prepackaged curriculum that deskilled them and frequently left them bored and reliant on outside experts and purchased material".[5] *De-skilling*: the second process distinguished by Apple, refers to the loss of skills due to the increase of simple executive routine-like and administrative tasks. Basically, what happens here is that a complicated task – teaching – that requires a high level of skills and knowledge is broken down into a large number of simpler tasks that do not need the same level of expertise and experience. This is Frederick Taylor's simplification of tasks. As teachers can presumably execute these simplified tasks much more efficiently than their initial, more complicated tasks, it is reasonable for their managers to expect teachers to be able to take on more tasks without needing compensation in the form of extra time or pay. This leads to a further *intensification* of their jobs – and this is the increase in production and efficiency envisaged by Taylor after implementing scientific management. Together, these three processes result in teachers having to do more simple tasks in the same amount of time, without having the opportunity to exert much influence on these tasks (i.e. loss of control). That is exactly what happened to factory workers in the late 1800s and early 1900s after the introduction of scientific management.

Lacking here is the idea that teachers should be paid for performance, for example, in the form of piece-rate systems or bonuses. However, doing so is certainly not impossible. In 2006–2009, a team of researchers from Vanderbilt University conducted a 3-year experiment in the Metropolitan Nashville School System.[6] They aimed to address "a significant problem in American education", namely "the absence of appropriate incentives" for teachers to teach well. Middle school mathematics teachers were randomly chosen for possible participation in the project, which focused on improvements of student performance on standardized mathematics tests. Teachers whose students showed large gains on these tests could earn a bonus of up to $15,000 on top of their regular yearly income. Smaller bonuses (of $5,000 and $10,000) were awarded for smaller gains. Teachers could decide for themselves what they would do to raise student performance. For example, they could seek coaching, participate in professional development activities, collaborate more with colleagues or simply reflect on their practices. As the researchers acknowledged with some regret, the effect of the possibility to earn a significant bonus on teacher performance was effectively nil: students of teachers who participated in the experiment (and who were eligible for receiving bonuses) did not do better than other students. Importantly, this example does not show that bonuses are ineffective in raising teacher performance or that teachers care little about receiving a fair income, but rather that it is quite possible to implement the pay-for-performance idea in the school context, just as can be done with the other principles stated by Taylor and his disciples.

Look around. Take any occupation and think about ways of implementing the principles of scientific management in that occupation. Chances are that these have already been implemented in some form. Setting production targets for obtaining a bonus; the introduction of new, simpler and more efficient ways of working (including the automatization and robotization of tasks); the presence of strict protocols and regulations to be attended to that limit an employee's control over his or her work; but also all sorts of procedures of selecting the right person for the job: such practices can all be interpreted in the light of the ongoing implementation of the principles so persuasively stated by Frederick Taylor.

By now, some of you may contend that in the last decades, much attention has been given to topics like worker empowerment, self-managing teams and the creation of flatter, less hierarchical organizations. Surely this has led to higher levels of control and, hence, better well-being for individual workers! Well, perhaps, but perhaps not. The introduction of self-managing teams, flatter organizations, et cetera, does not necessarily lead to higher levels of control for individual workers, especially not if such reorganizations are accompanied with narrowly-defined production targets and the introduction of regulations and protocols to attend to. As stated earlier, such protocols restrict worker autonomy and omit the need for close supervision. Workers will now literally supervise themselves, but given the presence of well-specified production goals they have little leeway in granting themselves any freedom to deviate from the protocols. Hence, their level of autonomy will not increase.

I was once hired by a producer of potato chips who had reformed their packaging department. All foremen had been fired, and teams now decided for themselves about their work rosters. There was little else for them to decide about; packaging potato chips – putting 12 plastic bags in a carton box, sealing it and putting it on a pallet – is a pretty simple job. Although they now had more control over their jobs, the members of the teams had become *less* satisfied, complaining that (a) they had not asked for more control, (b) now that their jobs had been "enriched" with extra tasks, they had to have boring team meetings to discuss their rosters amongst each other, and (c) in spite of having more tasks, they did not earn a penny extra. They suspected that this reorganization was intended as a cutback (no foremen anymore), rather than as an attempt to increase their work pleasure (as they had been told) – and they may well have been right about that. This admittedly anecdotal evidence is supported by the findings of a Dutch review study on the effects of self-managing teams on employee well-being, concluding that "these studies provided surprisingly little ground for general conclusions with regard to the effects of self-managing teams on the well-being of team members".[7] The message here is: although organizations may argue that their interventions enlarge worker control, in practice such interventions may not have the desired effects on worker autonomy and well-being. They can even backfire, especially if workers experience the increased possibilities for job control as an additional task or if they suspect that such interventions actually serve a hidden management agenda. *As your employer, I want to make you happy* (Chapter 4): sometimes this is really just management-speak for *I want more efficiency and more profits for the organization*.

So this is why we work the way we work. The rationalization of working life promised to deliver and has resulted in all sorts of material benefits. What we do while at work largely derives from our willingness (that is, our *choice*) to let these benefits dictate the principles according to which we work. That is, efficiency and productivity come first; worker well-being, health and happiness only come in insofar as they may be affected by working or if they are beneficial for (or at least do not get in the way of) productivity and efficiency.

HOW CAN WORK PERFORMANCE AND WORKER WELL-BEING BE OPTIMIZED – AND AT WHAT COSTS?

Is it bad for us to let the organization of working life follow from the economic principles of productivity and efficiency? Well, that depends. As customers, we all value having the possibility of buying top products for bottom prices. Even the anti-capitalist protesters clashing with the riot police during the 2017 summit of the G20 in Hamburg, Germany, took selfies of themselves rampaging, using an Apple iPhone – that capitalist symbol *par excellence*. From a customer's point of view, the rationalization of labour is excellent, since this presumably leads to higher productivity and efficiency, and, hence, lower prices (yet more stuff for us to indulge in).

However, the material presented in Chapters 3 and 4 suggests that we, in our roles of workers, may weigh these developments differently. Having high levels of control over our work is important for our well-being. Having a meaningful job is important as well, but conducting all sorts of simple routine-like tasks does not do much for our feeling that we do important work. Further, we know that work intensification is a major contributor to experiencing high job demands, especially if accompanied with pay-for-performance systems (Chapter 3) or inadequate monetary compensation in general (Chapter 4). These chapters confirmed our second assumption that *the way we work is an important factor in determining the "outcomes" of a job*. On the basis of these psychological notions, it seems plausible that the ongoing rationalization of working life – less control, more intensification – will continue to exert pressure on the way we work, with possibly adverse consequences for worker health and well-being.

Psychology has been instrumental in shaping modern working life. In 1913, Hugo Münsterberg wrote that work psychologists were

> partisan neither of the salesman nor of the customer, neither of the capitalist nor of the laborer . . . neither Socialist nor anti-Socialist, neither hightariff man nor free-trader.[8]

To Münsterberg, psychology was just a way to help achieve the goals specified by various societal parties – labour unions or capitalists, he was impartial to that. However, since psychologists (and, more generally, consultants) were frequently hired (and paid) by organizations to advise them on streamlining their production processes, chances are that initially, psychology was primarily used to the advantage of organizations, rather than to that of their employees.

This changed to some degree in the 1930s through the 1960s, when psychologists-consultants acknowledged that more attention for the needs and desires of workers could be advantageous in promoting the interests of the organization, as stated by the happy-productive worker hypothesis (Chapter 3). This reasoning resolved the apparent contradiction between promoting worker productivity and promoting worker happiness, resulting in a large and still increasing body of research on the antecedents of happiness at work. The findings of this research support the third assumption of this book that *there is nothing intrinsically bad about working hard*. Basically, psychology has shown us both how work performance and worker well-being can be optimized, pointing to the role of job features that make a job more pleasurable (Chapter 4), to that of personal characteristics in relation to performance (Chapter 5), and that of recovery (Chapter 6). Simultaneously, psychology has also pointed to the costs of not attending to worker well-being in terms of lack of performance, well-being, health and motivation.

THINGS TO COME: PSYCHOLOGY AT WORK

When preparing this chapter, I conducted a small-scale, semistructured study among the members of my extended family on their ideas regarding their employment, asking them for their opinion regarding the future of their jobs. While the number of responses was quite reasonable (as said, my grandfather raised a family of ten, most of whom had children as well: I even included some of their and my own children), I cannot claim any sort of representativeness. Interestingly, few participants held low-level production-oriented jobs: many of them were consultants, worked in the services industry, were engineers or nurses and/or held a management position. Most of them said that they could not have obtained their job without the education they had received. But in order to arrive there, virtually all had followed additional courses and training after completing higher education, confirming the idea that life-long learning is necessary to remain employable. As regards the future, most participants expected changes to occur due to computerization. However, they were quite confident that these would impose no real threats to their jobs. As one of my cousins bragged: "People in my job will continue to be able to earn a living – with an extra slice of cheese".

Perhaps my respondents were just slightly overconfident regarding their future perspectives. People tend to be optimistic, even in the face of oncoming difficulties and challenges – and such challenges are certainly coming our way, having implications for both workers and psychologists. In 2014, Maria Peeters and her colleagues identified various areas in which change will occur.[9] Most important, the *nature of work* will continue to change. Since the mid-1970s, the developed economies have witnessed a vast increase in service sector working and a corresponding decline in manufacturing jobs. This is likely to continue in the future, which implies that the characteristics of the "average" job will continue to change as well, putting less emphasis on physical job characteristics but more on more mental demands. For workers and organizations, this trend implies that they should continue to invest in the knowledge and skills of the first. It is up to psychologists to study how workers can be motivated to invest in themselves to keep their KSAOs up-to-date, to devise training programmes that are effective and that meet the needs of employees and the organizations they work for, to adjust the selection procedures they offer to their clients and to keep track of the effects of job characteristics on the health, well-being and productivity of workers.

Second, the *characteristics of the workforce* will change as well. Some 50 years ago, most work organizations were fairly similar in terms of the demographic features of their workforce. Employees usually shared a similar ethnic background and worked for the same employer throughout their working lives. Currently, the workforce is often much more diverse in terms of age, gender, tenure, ethnic background, education, et cetera. In such circumstances, it is a major challenge for human resource officers to manage these differences between individuals and/or groups at work, thus contributing to the success of workers and organizations alike.

Finally, *organizations and the context in which they operate* will change. The ongoing trend towards further globalization will continue to affect our organizations and thus, their employees. Reorganizations, mergers, outsourcing, computerization, robotization and the further rationalization of companies will often be accompanied with the loss of jobs and changes in the nature of other jobs. Here, some challenges for psychologists include motivating workers to invest in their employability, the optimal design of new and redesign of current jobs or even organizations and the motivation of workers who have been involved in the umpteenth organizational change.

Lots of change here, but the upshot is that in the face of all these developments, work, worker productivity and worker well-being will remain central themes in the future. As this book has shown, psychological insights are indispensable in understanding how developments regarding work will affect worker productivity and well-being and how these latter two concepts can be optimized. In this sense, the material presented in this book supports the final assumption presented in Chapter 1 that *taking a psychological view on working life is essential in understanding how the balance between being highly productive and remaining healthy and happy can be optimized.* The times may be a-changin', but psychology is here to stay.

REFERENCES

CHAPTER 1

1 Marx, K., & Engels, F. (1848/1969). Manifesto of the communist party. In *Marx/Engels selected works* (Vol. 1, pp. 98–137). Moscow: Progress Publishers.

2 Barks, C. (1961). *Monsterville*. Retrieved 13 July 2016 from http://duckcom icsrevue.blogspot.nl/2013/05/monsterville.html

3 Roosevelt, T. (1899/1900). *The strenuous life: Essays and addresses*. New York, NY: The Century Company.

4 Basalla, G. (1988). *The evolution of technology*. Cambridge, UK: Cambridge University Press.

5 Peeters, M. C. W., Taris, T. W., & De Jonge, J. (2014). People at work. In M. C. W. Peeters, J. de Jonge, and T. W. Taris (Eds.), *An introduction to contemporary work performance* (pp. 3–30). Chichester, UK: Wiley-Blackwell.

6 Oxford Dictionaries. *Work*. Retrieved 13 July 2016 from www.oxforddiction aries.com/definition/english/work

7 Hippocrates (2013). Hippocratic corpus: Excerpts: On decorum (translated by J. Longrigg). *Academic Medicine*, 88, 80.

8 Vegetius (390). *De Re Militari*. Retrieved 14 July 2016 from www.digitalattic. org/home/war/vegetius

9 Weber, L. W. (2002). Georgius Agricola: Scholar, physician, scientist, entrepreneur, diplomat. *Toxicological Science*, 69, 292–294.

10 Carnevale, F., & Iavicoli, S. (2015). Bernardino Ramazzini (1633–1714): A visionary physician, scientist and communicator. *Occupational and Environmental Medicine, 72*, 2–3.

11 Crafts, N. F. R. (1985). *British economic growth during the industrial revolution.* New York, NY: Oxford University Press.

12 Goodman, R. (2014). *How to be a Victorian.* London, UK: Penguin.

13 *BBC History: Living and working conditions.* Retrieved 13 July 2016, from www.bbc. co.uk/schools/gcsebitesize/history/shp/britishsociety/livingworkingcon-ditionsrev1.shtml

14 Humphries, J. (2010). *Childhood and child labour in the British industrial revolution.* Cambridge, UK: Cambridge University Press.

CHAPTER 2

1 Fitch, J. A. (1989). *The steel workers.* Pittsburgh, PA: University of Pittsburgh Press.

2 Kanigel, R. (2005). *The one best way: Frederick Winslow Taylor and the enigma of efficiency.* Cambridge, MA: MIT Press.

3 Hoopes, J. (2003). *False prophets: The gurus who created modern management and why their ideas are bad for business today.* New York, NY: Basic Books.

4 Taylor, F. W. (1912/1947). *Hearings in 1912 before special Investigating Committee of House of Representatives.* New York, NY: Harper.

5 Taylor, F. W. (1911). *The principles of scientific management.* New York, NY: Harper.

6 Wrege, C. D. (1995). F. W. Taylor's lecture on management, 4 June 1907: An introduction. *Journal of Management History, 1*, 4–7.

7 Gilbreth, L. M. (1925). *The quest of the best way: A sketch of the life of Frank Bunker Gilbreth.* New York, NY: Society of Industrial Engineering.

8 Ford, D. N. (1995). Frank Gilbert, 1868–1924, American engineer. In E. J. McMurray, J. K. Kosek, and R. M. Valade (Eds.), *Notable twentieth-century scientists* (pp. 759–760). New York, NY: Gale.

9 Gilbreth, L. M. (1914). *The psychology of management: The function of the mind in determining, teaching and installing methods of least waste.* New York, NY: Sturgis & Walton.

10 Baumgart, A., & Neuhauser, D. (2009). Frank and Lillian Gilbreth: Scientific management in the operating room. *Quality and Safety in Health Care, 18*, 413–415.

11 Graham, L. D. (1998). *Managing on her own: Dr. Lillian Gilbreth and women's work in the interwar era.* Norcross, GA: Engineering & Management Press.

12 Wrege, C. D., & Hodgetts, R. M. (2000). Frederick W. Taylor's 1899 pig iron observations: Examining fact, fiction, and lessons for the new millennium. *Academy of Management Journal, 43,* 1283–1291.

13 Locke, E. A. (1982). The ideas of Frederick W. Taylor: An evaluation. *Academy of Management Review, 7,* 14–24.

14 Streitfelt, D. (2015). Data-crunching is coming to help your boss manage your time. *New York Times,* 17 August.

CHAPTER 3

1 Roethlisberger, F. J., & Dickson, W. J. (1939). *Management and the worker.* Cambridge, MA: Harvard University Press.

2 Levitt, S. D., & List, J. A. (2009). Was there really a Hawthorne effect at the Hawthorne plant? An analysis of the original illumination experiments. *American Economic Journal: Applied Economics, 3,* 224–238.

3 Mayo, E. (1945). *The social problems of an industrial civilization.* Boston, MA: Harvard University.

4 Sonnenveld, J. A. (1985). Shedding light on the Hawthorne studies. *Journal of Occupational Behavior, 6,* 111–130.

5 Jenkins, G. D., Mitra, A., Gupta, N., & Shaw, J. D. (1998). Are financial incentives related to performance? A meta-analytical review of empirical research. *Journal of Applied Psychology, 83,* 777–787.

6 Levitt, S. D., & Neckermann, S. (2014). What field experiments have and have not taught us about managing workers. *Oxford Review of Economic Policy, 30,* 639–657.

7 Freeman, R. B., & Kleiner, M. M. (2005). The last American shoe manufacturers: Decreasing productivity and increasing profits in the shift from piece rates to continuous flow production. *Industrial Relations, 44,* 307–330.

8 Organ, D. W., Podsakoff, P. M., & MacKenzie, S. P. (2006). *Organisational citizenship behavior: Its nature, antecedents, and consequences.* London, UK: Sage.

9 Taylor, F. W. (1911). *The principles of scientific management.* New York, NY: Harper.

10 Johansson, B., Rask, R., & Stenberg, M. (2010). Piece rates and their effects on health and safety: A literature review. *Applied Ergonomics, 41,* 607–614.

11 Hersey, R. B. (1932). *Workers' emotions in shop and home: A study of individual workers from the psychological and physiological standpoint.* Philadelphia: University of Pennsylvania Press.

12 Judge, T. A., Thoresen, C. J., Bono, J. E., & Patton, G. K. (2001). The job satisfaction-job performance relationship: A qualitative and quantitative review. *Psychological Bulletin, 127,* 376–407.

13 Riketta, M. (2008). The causal relation between job attitudes and performance: A meta-analysis of panel studies. *Journal of Applied Psychology, 93,* 472–481.

14 Ohly, S., Sonnentag, S., Niessen, C., & Zapf, D. (2010). Diary studies in organisational research: An introduction and some practical recommendations. *Journal of Personnel Psychology, 9,* 79–93.

15 Schaufeli, W. B., Leiter, M. P., & Maslach, C. (2009). Burnout: 35 years of research and practice. *Career Development International, 14,* 204–2020.

16 Swider, B. W., & Zimmerman, R. D. (2010). Born to burnout: A meta-analytic path model of personality, job burnout, and work outcomes. *Journal of Vocational Behavior, 76,* 487–506.

17 Taris, T. W. (2006). Is there a relationship between burnout and objective performance? A critical review of 16 studies. *Work & Stress, 20,* 316–334.

18 Salanova, M., Agut, S., & Peiro, J. M. (2005). Linking organisational resources and work engagement to employee performance and customer loyalty: The mediation of service climate. *Journal of Applied Psychology, 90,* 1217–1227.

19 Harter, J. K., Schmidt, F. L., & Hayes, T. L. (2001). Business-unit-level relationship between employee satisfaction, employee engagement, and business outcomes: A meta-analysis. *Journal of Applied Psychology, 87,* 268–279.

20 Levine, D., Toffel, M., & Johnson, M. (2012). Randomized government safety inspections reduce worker injuries with no detectable job loss. *Science, 336,* 907–911.

21 European Agency for Safety and Health at Work. (2014). *The business case for safety and health at work: Cost-benefit analyses of interventions in small and medium-sized enterprises.* Luxembourg: EU-OSHA.

CHAPTER 4

1 Hackman, J. R., & Oldham, G. R. (1980). *Work redesign.* Reading, MA: Addison-Wesley.

2 Wall, T. D., Clegg, C. G., & Jackson, P. R. (1978). An evaluation of the Job Characteristics model. *Journal of Occupational Psychology*, 51, 183–196.

3 Fried, Y., & Ferris, G. R. (1987). The validity of the Job Characteristics model: A review and meta-analysis. *Personnel Psychology*, 40, 287–322.

4 Karasek, R. A. (1976). *The impact of the work environment on life outside the job* [unpublished PhD thesis]. Cambridge, MA: MIT Press.

5 Karasek, R. A., & Theorell, T. (1990). *Healthy work: Stress, productivity, and the reconstruction of working life*. New York, NY: Basic Books.

6 Hausser, J. A., Mojzisch, A., Niesel, M., & Schulz-Hardt, S. (2010). Ten years on: A review of recent research on the Job Demand-Control(-Support) model and psychological well-being. *Work & Stress*, 24, 1–35.

7 Madsen, I. E., Nyberg, S. I., Magnusson Hanson, L. L., Ferrie, J. E., Ahola, K., et al. (2017). Job strain as a risk factor for clinical depression: Systematic review and meta-analysis with additional individual participant data. *Psychological Medicine*, 47, 1342–1356.

8 Siegrist, J. (2008). Effort-reward imbalance and health in a globalized economy. *Scandinavian Journal of Work, Environment, and Health*, 34, 163–168.

9 Van Vegchel, N., De Jonge, J., Bosma, H., & Schaufeli, W. B. (2005). Reviewing the effort-reward imbalance model: Drawing up the balance of 45 empirical studies. *Social Science and Medicine*, 60, 1117–1131.

10 Eddy, P., Heckenberg, R., Wertheim, E. H., Kent, S., & Wright, B. J. (2016). A systematic review and meta-analysis of the Effort-Reward Imbalance model of workplace stress with indicators of immune function. *Journal of Psychosomatic Research*, 91, 1–8.

11 Warr, P. (2013). Jobs and job-holders: Two sources of happiness and unhappiness. In S. A. David, I. Boniwell, and A. C. Ayers (Eds.), *The Oxford handbook of happiness* (pp. 733–750). Oxford, UK: Oxford University Press.

12 Demerouti, E., Bakker, A. B., Nachreiner, F., & Schaufeli, W. B. (2001). The Job Demands-Resources model of burnout. *Journal of Applied Psychology*, 86, 499–512.

13 Taris, T. W. (2017). Models in work and health research: the JDC(S), ERI and JD-R frameworks. In R. J. Burke and K. M. Page (Eds.), *Research handbook on work and well-being* (pp. 77–98). Cheltenham, UK: Elgar.

14 Deci, E. L., & Ryan, R. M. (2000). The "what" and "why" of goal pursuits: Human needs and the self-determination of behavior. *Psychological Inquiry*, 11, 227–268.

15 Gagné, M., & Deci, E. (2005). Self-determination theory and work motivation. *Journal of Organisational Behavior*, 26, 331–362.

16 De Cooman, R., Stynen, D., Van den Broeck, A., Sels, L., & De Witte, H. (2013). How job characteristics relate to need satisfaction and autonomous motivation: Implications for work effort. *Journal of Applied Social Psychology*, 43, 1342–1352.

17 Van der Elst, T., Van den Broeck, A., De Witte, H., & De Cuyper, N. (2012). The mediating role of frustration of psychological needs in the relationship between job insecurity and work-related well-being. *Work & Stress*, 26, 252–271.

18 Van Beek, I., Hu, Q., Schaufeli, W. B., Taris, T. W., & Schreurs, B. H. J. (2012). For fun, love, or money: What drives workaholic, engaged, and burned-out employees at work? *Applied Psychology: An International Review*, 61, 30–55.

CHAPTER 5

1 Taylor, F. W. (1911). *The principles of scientific management*. New York, NY: Harper.

2 Blatter, J. T. (2014). *The psychotechnics of everyday life: Hugo Münsterberg and the politics of applied psychology, 1887–1917*. Cambridge, MA: Harvard University.

3 Münsterberg, H. (1913). *Psychology and industrial efficiency*. Boston, MA: Houghton Mifflin.

4 Parsons, F. (1909). *Choosing a vocation*. Boston, MA: Houghton Mifflin.

5 Guion, R. M., & Gottier, R. F. (1965). Validity of personality measures in personnel selection. *Personnel Psychology*, 18, 135–164.

6 McCrae, R. R., & John, O. P. (1992). An introduction to the five-factor model and its applications. *Journal of Personality*, 60, 175–215.

7 Barrick, M. R., & Mount, M. K. (1991). The big five personality dimensions and job performance: A meta-analysis. *Personnel Psychology*, 44, 1–26.

8 Rothstein, M. G., & Goffin, R. D. (2006). The use of personality measures in personnel selection: What does current research support? *Human Resource Management Review*, 16, 155–180.

9 Hunter, J. E., & Schmidt, F. L. (1996). Intelligence and job performance: Economic and social implications. *Psychology, Public Policy, and Law*, 2, 447–472.

10 See Hunter, J. E. (1986). Cognitive ability, cognitive aptitudes, job knowledge, and job performance. *Journal of Vocational Behavior*, 29, 340–362; and Hunter, J. E., & Hunter, R. F. (1984). Validity and utility of alternative predictors of job performance. *Psychological Bulletin*, 96, 72–98.

11 Van Rooy, D., & Viswesvaran, C. (2004). Emotional intelligence: A meta-analytic investigation of predictive validity and nomological net. *Journal of Vocational Behavior, 65*, 71–95.

12 Wilderom, C. P. M., Hur, Y. H., Wiersma, U. J., Van den Berg, P. T., & Lee, J. (2015). From manager's emotional intelligence to objective store performance: Through store cohesiveness and sales-directed employee behavior. *Journal of Organisational Behavior, 36*, 825–844.

13 O'Boyle, E. H., Humphrey, R. H., Pollack, J. M., Hawver, T. H., & Story, P. H. (2015). The relation between emotional intelligence and job performance: A meta-analysis. *Journal of Organisational Behavior, 32*, 788–818.

14 Macan, T. (2009). The employment interview: A review of current studies and directions for future research. *Human Resource Management Review, 19*, 203–218.

15 Wagner, R. (1949). The employment interview: A critical summary. *Personnel Psychology, 2*, 17–46.

16 McDaniel, M. A., Whetzel, D. L., Schmidt, F. L., & Maurer, S. D. (1994). The validity of employment interviews: A comprehensive review and meta-analysis. *Journal of Applied Psychology, 79*, 599–616.

17 Hoffman, B. J., Kennedy, C. L., LoPilato, A. C., Monahan, E. L., & Lance, C. E. (2015). A review of the content, criterion-related, and construct-related validity of assessment centers. *Journal of Applied Psychology, 100*, 1143–1168.

18 Schmidt, F. L., & Hunter, J. E. (1998). The validity and utility of selection methods in Personnel Psychology: Practical and theoretical implications of 85 years of research findings. *Psychological Bulletin, 124*, 262–274.

19 Blume, B. D., Ford, J. K., Baldwin, T. T., & Huang, J. L. (2010). Transfer of training: A meta-analytic review. *Journal of Management, 36*, 1065–1105.

CHAPTER 6

1 Caesar, J. (2013). *The civil war* (sections 3.90–3.99). Translated in English by W. A. McDeVitte and W. S. Bohn. Hastings, UK: Delphi Classics.

2 Taylor, F. W. (1911). *The principles of scientific management*. New York, NY: Harper.

3 Graham, L. D. (1999). Domesticating efficiency: Lillian Gilbreth's scientific management of homemakers, 1924–1930. *Signs, 24*, 633–675.

4 See Eurofound. (2016). *Sixth European working conditions survey*. Luxembourg: Publications Office of the European Union; and Bureau of Labor Statistics.

(2015). *The employment situation – February 2015*. Washington, DC: Department of Labor.

5 Hu, N. C., Chen, J. D., & Cheng, T. J. (2016). The associations between long working hours, physical inactivity, and burnout. *Journal of Occupational and Environmental Medicine, 58,* 514–518.

6 Kivimäki, M., Jokela, M., Nyberg, S.T., Singh-Manoux, A., Fransson, E. I., et al. (2015). Long working hours and risk of coronary heart disease and stroke: A systematic review and meta-analysis of published and unpublished data for 603 838 individuals. *The Lancet, 386,* 1710–1711.

7 Bannai, A., & Tamakoshi, A. (2014). The association between long working hours and health: A systematic review of epidemiological evidence. *Scandinavian Journal of Work, Environment, and Health, 40,* 5–18.

8 Schluter, P. J., Turner, C., & Benefer, C. (2012). Long working hours and alcohol risk among Australian and New Zealand nurses and midwives: A cross-sectional study. *International Journal of Nursing Studies, 49,* 701–709.

9 Folkard, S., & Lombardi, D. A. (2006). Modeling the impact of the components of long work hours on injuries and "accidents". *American Journal of Industrial Medicine, 49,* 953–963.

10 Pencavel, J. (2015). The productivity of working hours. *The Economic Journal, 125,* 2052–2076.

11 See Ganster, D. C., Rosen, C. C., & Fisher, G. G. (in press). Long working hours and well-being: What we know, what we do not know, and what we need to know. *Journal of Management*; and Bernstrom, V., & Houkes, I. (in press). A systematic literature review of the relationship between work hours and sickness absence. *Work & Stress.*

12 Meijman, T. F., & Mulder, G. (1998). Psychological aspects of workload. In P. J. Drenth, H. Thierry, and C. J. de Wolff (Eds.), *Handbook of work and organisational psychology* (pp. 5–33). Hove, UK: Psychology Press.

13 Geurts, S. A. E., & Sonnentag, S. (2006). Recovery as an explanatory mechanism in the relation between acute stress reactions and chronic health impairment. *Scandinavian Journal of Work, Environment and Health, 32,* 482–492.

14 Tucker, P. (2003). The impact of rest breaks upon accident risk, fatigue and performance: A review. *Work & Stress, 17,* 123–127.

15 Lombardi, D. A., Jin, K., Courtney, T. K., Arlinghaus, A., Folkard, S., Liang, Y., and Perry, M. J. (2014). The effects of rest breaks, work shift start time, and sleep on the onset of severe injury among workers in the People's Republic of China. *Scandinavian Journal of Work, Environment and Health, 40,* 146–155.

16 Kim, S., Park, Y., & Niu, Q. (2017). Micro-break activities at work to recover from daily job demands. *Journal of Organisational Behavior*, 38, 22–44.

17 Genaidy, A. M., Delgado, E., & Bustos, E. (1995). Active microbreak effects on musculoskeletal comfort ratings in meatpacking plants. *Ergonomics*, 38, 326–336.

18 Sonnentag, S., Venz, L., & Casper, A. (2017). Advances in recovery research: What have we learned? What should be done next? *Journal of Occupational Health Psychology*, 22, 365–380.

19 Greenhaus, J. H., & Beutell, N. J. (1985). Sources and conflict between work and family roles. *Academy of Management Review*, 10, 76–88. Note that experiences at work and home can also strengthen one's functioning in both contexts, for example when the skills learned in one context (such as time management skills) improve one's functioning in the other. This is referred to as *work-home enhancement*.

20 De Bloom, J., Geurts, S. A. E., Sonnentag, S., Taris, T., De Weerth, C., & Kompier, M. A. J. (2008). How does a vacation from work affect employee health and well-being? *Psychology & Health*, 26, 1606–1622.

CHAPTER 7

1 Frey, C. B., & Osborne, M. (2013). *The future of employment: How susceptible are jobs to computerisation?* Oxford, UK: University of Oxford.

2 Brown, P., Hesketh, A., & Williams, S. (2003). Employability in a knowledge-driven economy. *Journal of Education and Work*, 16, 107–126.

3 Luiten van Zanden, J., Baten, J., Foldvari, P., & Van Leeuwen, B. (2014). The changing shape of global inequality 1820–2000: Exploring a new data set. *The Review of Income and Wealth*, 60, 279–297.

4 Apple, M. W. (1986). *Teachers and texts: A political economy of class and gender relations in education.* London, UK: Routledge.

5 Apple, M. W., & Jungck, S. (1990). "You don't have to be a teacher to teach this unit": Teaching, technology and gender in the classroom. *American Educational Research Journal*, 27, 227–251.

6 Springer, M. G., Ballou, D., Hamilton, L., Le, V., Lockwood, J. R., McCaffrey, D., Pepper, M., & Stecher, B. (2010). *Teacher pay for performance: Experimental evidence from the Project on Incentives in Teaching.* Nashville, TN: Vanderbilt University.

7 Van Mierlo, H., Rutte, C. G., Kompier, M. A. J., & Doorewaard, H. C. A. M. (2004). A theoretical and methodological analysis of empirical studies on

psychological well-being in self-managing teams [in Dutch]. *Gedrag & Organisatie, 17,* 43–58.

8 Münsterberg, H. (1913). *Psychology and industrial efficiency.* Boston, MA: Houghton Mifflin.

9 Peeters, M. C. W., Taris, T. W., & De Jonge, J. (2014). People at work. In M. C. W. Peeters, J. de Jonge, and T. W. Taris (Eds.), *An introduction to contemporary work psychology* (pp. 3–30). Chichester, UK: Wiley-Blackwell.

Printed in the United States
by Baker & Taylor Publisher Services